BETTER HEALTH
WITH FOOT
REFLEXOLOGY
THE INGHAM METHOD ® OF REFLEXOLOGY

BETTER HEALTH
WITH FOOT
REFLEXOLOGY

THE INGHAM METHOD ® OF REFLEXOLOGY

by
Dwight C. Byers

Your quest for health will be enhanced
by having read this book.

INGHAM PUBLISHING, INC. • PUBLISHER
Saint Petersburg • Florida • U.S.A.

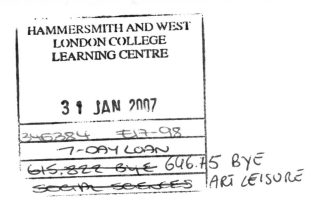
Copyright © 2001 by Dwight C. Byers

ISBN-1-891130-00-5
Revised Edition, for 2001
from the original edition 1983
3rd printing - 2006
Published and Distributed Throughout the World by
INGHAM PUBLISHING, INC • PUBLISHER
PO Box 12642
St. Petersburg, Florida 33733-2642, U.S.A.
Phone: (727) 343-4811   Fax: (727) 381- 2807
website: www.reflexology-usa.net
Printed in the United States of America

iv

Dedicated to
Eunice D. Ingham
(February 24, 1889 to December 10, 1974)
The founder of Foot Reflexology

My aunt and my mentor,
She remains my inspiration.

ACKNOWLEDGMENTS

I would like to acknowledge the very valuable help and assistance from those patient souls who provided me with direction and solace as well as rekindling my enthusiasm and determination.

Their dedicated help made all this possible.

To my wife, Nancy, who was my chief critic and editor and who set the goals as well as supplying the encouragement to reach them. Thank you for all your work and guidance in the revision of this book.

To Dick Shannon, professional medical writer, who guided my pen over many a rough paragraph into the intricacies of the human body for the original book.

To John Bloch, a very patient and talented artist, for his many hours of sketching and illustrating the original edition. A special thank you for the many hours spent adding the graphics to the new photos, preparing the layout of this revised book and designing the new cover for this revision.

To Lilian Tibshraeny, a special thank you for the many hours, days, weeks and months of dedicated work for Reflexology and the text revision, along with the new photos, for this revised book.

To my grandson, James Pedersen, for his dedication to Reflexology in being the perfect foot model for this book. Thank you for your love and patience.

To Kelley Lough, for her beautiful hands and patience during the photo shoot for this book. Thank you for the many hours of typing and poof reading.

To Tony Porter of London, England for his invaluable suggestions.

To Ray C. Wunderlich, Jr., M.D. for his professional perusal and suggestions in many technical areas.

To Gary Fleischman, D.P.M., Arthur Pauls, D.O. , and Jack Vinson, D. O. for their encouragement.

To the office staff of Ingham Publishing and International Institute for their aid.

To my sister, Eusebia B. Messenger, R.N. for your encouragement.

My gratitude to all of you for a job well done.

FOREWORD

Reflexology stands the test of patient acceptance as a valid means of making one feel good, relaxing, and functioning better than he otherwise would. As such, Reflexology qualifies as an important adjunct for health care. As in the case with any therapeutic modality, the skill, enthusiasm and personality of the therapist are important variables in determining the effectiveness of the treatment.

One could imagine studies in which patients would be assigned to several groups: one group to receive acupuncture of the feet, another acupressure of the feet, another massage of the feet, and a final group to receive Ingham-Byers Reflexology. Other more sophisticated tests could be fashioned. Such studies might end up showing all methods to be helpful.

For whatever reasons, we do know that clients receiving Reflexology sessions feel better, function better and often improve in the biological and psycho-social disorders that lead them to seek help. It is entirely possible that Reflexology works for reasons other than those usually attributed to this helpful methodology. The laying on of hands does have special significance for most persons. Laying hands on the feet probably elicits greater relaxation than laying hands on any other body area. Therapeutic touch for health has been shown to be a valid help for persons who hurt and there is no reason that touch for health on the feet should be an exception. The special method of Reflexology developed by Eunice Ingham and followed faithfully by her knowledgeable nephew, Dwight Byers, is impressive in its ability to facilitate healing in the body.

Quite probably, it will eventually be shown that Reflexology alters energy flow in the body. Hang ups in energy flow are, in all likelihood, removed. Restriction of blood and lymphatic flow to certain regions of the body may be normalized.

The feet are at the extreme end of the body. Farthest from the heart, blood and lymph from the feet must flow uphill against gravity. Movement of these vital liquids is essential. As with any stream, heavy particles will tend to settle out as sediment, especially when the current is not swift. Also, sluggish flow may promote poor oxygenation of tissues and inadequate removal of waste. Sludging of blood may occur, further hindering blood flow.

There are 7,200 nerve endings in each foot. Perhaps this fact, more than any other, explains why we feel so much better when our feet are worked using Reflexology. Nerve endings in the feet have extensive interconnections through the spinal cord and brain with all areas of the body. Surely the feet are a gold mine of opportunity to release tension and enhance health. The Ingham-Byers method of Reflexology deserves wide usage as a valuable adjunct to the medical care of patients in need.

Ray C. Wunderlich Jr., M.D.

Ray C. Wunderlich Jr., M.D.
Preventive Medicine and Health Promotion, St. Petersburg, Florida

FOREWORD

Good health is so precious that every possible means to achieve this state must be considered and applied. The science of Reflexology developed as one of these means, by which special, learned techniques locate exactly where disorders occur, and then returns normal function to the respective tissues and organs.

I have been associated with Reflexology for over a decade, and I apply it in my practice for rehabilitation of disabilities. As a Doctor of Pediatric Medicine, I always search for improved methods of treatment for the betterment of my patients. I find in Reflexology relief and elimination of many disorders that otherwise would remain uncorrected. Medication, surgery, acupuncture, bio-mechanics and physical therapy comprise much of my work, yet Reflexology continues to be an essential aid either by itself or with other modes of therapy.

Dwight C. Byers wrote this updated volume from years of experience and dedicated research. He offers scientific descriptions and easy-to-follow applications not available in any other book dealing with this subject. Delightful down-to-earth comments and personal explanations create an imagined sense of attending a Reflexology seminar. Still the same tradition of professional writing standards, found in books by Eunice Ingham, exist here to be enjoyed with educational benefit by people in all fields of health. The book not only covers techniques of working both feet and hands, but also, as related to Reflexology, it describes anatomy and physiology of body systems, disease processes and referral areas between the upper and lower torso and extremities.

It is my hope that my medical and surgical colleagues will see the proven value of Reflexology as an effective disease-fighting method. For the end result strives to provide wholesome, long life for us all.

Sincerely,
Gary F. Fleischman, D.P.M.

Member of American Podiatry Association
Member of Connecticut Podiatry Association
Member of American Public Health Association
Member of American Academy of Podiatric Acupuncture
Member of United States Congressional Advisory Board
Served two terms as Chairman of the Board of Health, Milford, Connecticut

FOREWORD

It gives me great pleasure to write this foreword for my friend, Dwight Byers. I first met Dwight during a lecture tour I was making of the U.S.A. in 1976. I, as the founder of Ortho-Bionomy, was introducing my therapy to see if there was an interest for yet another new form of body work.

While in Houston, I took a seminar on Reflexology conducted by Dwight Byers. He taught it with great clarity and understanding of the subject and I was very impressed by his knowledge and experience, coupled with many years of research into the therapy.

I personally feel that Reflexology should be learned by everyone who wants to understand the reflexes of the body. With this training, a person may easily move on and learn other forms of reflex work, such as Ortho-Bionomy and find they learn more rapidly, because the learning of Reflexology (as taught by Mr. Byers) gives a person the necessary touch needed in healing.

The system of Reflexology is safe, yet extremely effective in many cases where other therapies have failed to bring results. I use the technique often in my general practice of Ortho-Bionomy and Osteopathy.

I would remind the reader that however good a book is, it becomes better when the study of it is coupled with practical experience. This is gained in a seminar given by someone who not only fully understands the subject, but who, like Dwight Byers, has the 'knack' of making the good work both educational and interesting.

Reflexology today is growing by leaps and bounds and the teaching of it, due to Mr. Byers and carefully selected assistants, is showing persons in all walks of life that it is possible to help ourselves and our fellow man.

I feel Reflexology is one of the real natural alternatives that can only make any other therapy better by its inclusion into any healing program.

Dwight Byers is a tireless worker and is a credit to this alternative field of healing. I feel he is doing a great service to mankind in his educational approach to health, not only in the therapeutic line, but in the preventative field as well.

I trust this book will aid those whose interest lies in this field and give my best wishes to you all.

Love and blessings,
Arthur Lincoln Pauls, D.O.

Doctor of Osteopathy and Founder of Ortho-Bionomy
Herts, England

FOREWORD

I have been acquainted with Reflexology since the summer of 1952 when I was a student at Kirksville College of Osteopathic Medicine. Eunice Ingham conducted a two week teaching seminar for all who were interested in the location of the reflexes on each foot and the corresponding areas which are related to other parts of the body. She untiringly demonstrated her ability to work these reflex areas in the feet.

During the next two years I visited several large cities where Miss Ingham was holding seminars and teaching this technique to mostly lay people, some chiropractors and a few physicians. I talked with many people and heard many accounts of people with various forms of ill health who were helped tremendously with frequent Reflexology manipulative therapy.

My own experience with this modality has been very interesting. Many times I have elicited intense reflexes on the feet which correlated to known pathological conditions within the patient's body. Many of these people acquired relief from their discomfort after working the reflex area in the feet.

This technique of Reflexology should be taught to all professional, and especially non-professional people who have a desire to seek treatment for bodily ailments other than, or even in conjunction with, orthodox medical approaches to illness.

I am pleased to recommend this book and the teachings of Dwight C. Byers in the application of Reflexology.

Jack R. Vinson D.O.

Jack R. Vinson, D.O.
Dallas, Texas

PREFACE

When faced with the question of "Why this book?", I hesitate to answer for fear that I may not adequately answer **all** the reasons.

But perhaps a few will suffice for now.

The first, and, I feel the most compelling reason is the simple and rather obvious fact that the time has come to establish (or should I say "re-establish") those basic tenets put forth so clearly by my aunt, Eunice Ingham, in her two books: *Stories the Feet Can Tell Thru Reflexology* and *Stories the Feet Have Told Thru Reflexology*. These books, together with her seminar teaching and original research, clearly establish her as the founder and mother of Reflexology as it is known today.

For some years, these books remained the basic guideline to the science of Reflexology. They were a basic history of her work as she struggled to evolve this most interesting approach to better health. Anyone who has read through these two books suddenly realizes that Eunice Ingham did add the needed dimensions of knowledge and the impetus in making Reflexology work.

Over 65 years of our research and experience Reflexology has advanced to what it is today. We are able to provide the highest standard of teaching excellence based on this knowledge and experience. It is up to the serious student to research and find a school with the proper credentials and who is serious about the art of Reflexology. A point to remember is that Reflexology works; it is much like a computer . . . the computer always works if the operator has the ability to elicit the correct information.

Today, having read many books on this subject I realize that Reflexology has been combined with other modalities. Reflexology can be used with other modalities such as body massage, aroma therapy, acupressure, auricular therapy, etc. but they are all separate modalities and should not be considered Reflexology.

I have always held my Aunt's view that Reflexology is a science. True, it is one in which we do not know *all* the answers . . . but nevertheless, it is a science that should not be exploited to the point where reason is abandoned for pure gain.

This has led me to write this book. I want it to be the **most complete** and **authoritative** reference manual available on the subject of Reflexology.

It has not been an easy task. I have spent much time poring over my Aunt's original writings, correspondence and notes . . . from these, has evolved the second reason for this book.

My second purpose in developing this book is the very same as the one I use in teaching seminars on Reflexology to thousands of students at hundreds of seminars . . . to continue to develop Reflexology as a science by sharing my knowledge of the subject with those who seriously consider the goals of Reflexology to be that of helping their fellow human beings.

This was the basic goal of Eunice Ingham . . . as it remains mine today . . . to help mankind as much as we are able whenever possible and wherever we might be. This goal has been partially reached through our many seminars and the distribution of bulletins from the *International Institute of Reflexology*®. Now, with the publication of this book we are able to communicate on an even greater scale and in far greater depth.

But the message remains the same . . . Reflexology is not a commodity for sale; rather, it is a dedication to a single purpose . . . bringing help and better health to our fellow humans in a natural way.

If you share this dedication and become a Reflexologist . . . let it be your goal, today, tomorrow and for all your tomorrows.

But we caution you to remember that Reflexology is constantly changing . . . everything is not in this book, nor *any* book. The secret to becoming a successful Reflexologist is continued education and practice.

Practice doesn't make perfect . . . perfect practice makes perfect . . . continuing to update your education makes practice more perfect. And as you progress through the information presented in this book, you will learn the truth in my favorite adage, "Experience is the Father of All Knowledge".

Dwight C. Byers

A NOTE TO THE READER

This book and its contents and opinions are the result of extensive experience in foot Reflexology and represent the theories of the author who is not a medical doctor. There may be some sections and opinions which are not in conformance to the theories and practice of the medical profession. The author and publisher strongly suggest that self diagnosis not be attempted based on symptoms delineated in this book. The symptoms as described in this book may be indicative of more than one condition within the body.

In any case of illness or even symptoms of a bodily dysfunction, it is advisable and essential that a competent medical practitioner be consulted.

It should also be noted that Reflexology is **not** a panacea . . . it is an adjunct to medicine and must be regarded as such. Foot and hand Reflexology have become a well known modality of Integrative Medicine today.

CONTENTS

HISTORY OF REFLEXOLOGY

"Beloved, I wish above all things that thou mayest prosper and be in health, even as thy soul prospereth."

3 John 2

EGYPTIAN REFLEXOLOGY TREATMENT

Early sixth dynasty, about 2,330 B.C. wall painting in tomb of Ankhmahor (highest official after the king) at Saqqara, and is known as the physicians tomb. Translation reads: "Don't hurt me." The practitioner's reply: "I shall act so you praise me."

HISTORY OF REFLEXOLOGY

Not being a qualified explorer of antiquity, I must allow those who are far better equipped than myself to study the origin of this science of Reflexology. I will only add this small contribution to their search: its origin evidently reaches back into ancient Egypt as evidenced by inscriptions found in a physician's tomb (*mastaba*) in Egypt. The hieroglyphics and their translation are shown on **page 2**.

Just what relationship Reflexology, as we know it today, has with the very ancient art of Oriental Pressure Therapy is still unknown. There would seem to be quite a distinct relationship between the two sciences; my own personal feeling is that it does serve as a link to the ancient art as practiced by the early Egyptians. Then, of course, we read in the Bible of the traditions associated with the feet, that of washing them, etc. Could this be another historical hint?

There are just too many coincidences to gloss over when studying the history of our science today, but once again let me add that I am not a medical historian so I will leave those clues to others who delve into the dim past.

The trip through time to our present age is a somewhat different matter. My initiation into Reflexology came as a youth when I served as one of the *guinea pigs* for my aunt, Eunice Ingham, as she was developing the Ingham Method® of Reflexology. But more of these experiences later.

I suppose that anyone who wanted to study the history of modern Reflexology should begin with Doctor William H. Fitzgerald.

The reason why I chose to begin with this gentleman becomes clear as the result of a search through the faded, yellow newspaper clippings of my Aunt Eunice. One of the clippings is dated April 29, 1934; and the headline reads:

MYSTERY OF ZONE THERAPY EXPLAINED

The article tells of a dinner party at which one of the guests was Dr. William H. Fitzgerald, touted as "the discoverer of zone therapy".

In 1917, Dr. Fitzgerald published a most interesting book with the title *Zone Therapy, or Relieving Pain at Home*. In the book, he describes his success with relieving pain through the use of various devices on the hands and fingers.

It so happened that at that fateful dinner was a well-known concert singer who had announced that the upper register tones of her voice had gone flat and the article noted that throat specialists had been unable to discover the cause of this affliction. Dr. Fitzgerald, according to the newspaper article, asked to examine the fingers and toes of the singer. After his examination, he told her that the cause of the loss of her upper tones was attributed to a callus on her right great toe. After applying pressure to the corresponding part in the same zone for a few minutes, the patient remarked that the pain in her toe had disappeared. Then, to quote from the article, "whereupon the doctor asked her to try the tones of the upper register. Miraculously, it seemed to us, the singer reached two notes higher than she had ever sung before."

Incredible?

Perhaps to the reporter writing that story, but to one who was under the tutelage of my Aunt Eunice, it was an everyday occurrence.

But what did that dinner party, held so many years ago, have to do with our current concepts of Reflexology?

Dr. Fitzgerald was a physician at the Boston City Hospital as well as a practicing Laryngologist at St. Francis Hospital in Hartford, Connecticut. He had also studied in Vienna, as well as other places in Europe, and was on the staff of the Central London Ears, Nose and Throat Hospital for two years. It was in 1902, while he was head of the Nose and Throat Department, that he became acquainted with zone therapy. He worked with the hands by applying pressure to various parts of the fingers in order to relieve pain. It should be noted here that he used a variety of appliances . . . but it *was* quite successful.

The seed was planted; the beginnings of what we know today as Reflexology were fundamentally written in that book. The book itself made no great impact on the medical world and gathered dust on many a physician's shelf . . . except for one who was intrigued by this theory of zone therapy, the physician was Dr. Joe Shelby Riley.

To him, it presented a distinct possibility which ought to be explored. He expressed his thoughts to his staff therapist. The seed started to grow.

And working as a therapist in his office was one Eunice Ingham.

Dr. Riley became interested in the work being done by Dr. Fitzgerald but did not actively pursue it. Eunice Ingham was also interested in zone therapy because of the extensive work she was doing as a therapist. They had discussed the theory many times until the desire to know more about the theory became almost an obsession with Eunice Ingham. She knew that Fitzgerald concentrated mainly on the hands with his theory . . . but, if the hands responded to this treatment . . . there was one other corresponding part of the body which was even more sensitive . . . the foot. After explaining this theory to Dr. Riley and gaining encouragement from him, she began to develop her foot Reflexology theory in the early 1930's.

She began probing the feet . . . finding a tender spot and equating it with the anatomy of the body . . . mapping ever so carefully the zones of the feet in relation to the organs of the body.

So then she started working on people's feet using the thumb to press upon certain areas . . . probing and constantly looking for tender spots . . . remembering that Fitzgerald *had* in one section of his book drawn a rudimentary body upon the feet. It is important here to note that Dr. Fitzgerald had recommended using rubber bands, combs, etc. on the fingers and the hands to deaden the pain for an anesthesia effect. Eunice Ingham did not follow this advice. By constantly probing with her fingers and thumbs, she did manage to locate the tender areas on the feet. One early method she experimented with was to locate the tender spots and then to tape wads of cotton over these spots and have the person walk upon them. This system over-stimulated the reflexes and caused some reactions. At this point she found it more helpful to use the thumb and fingers to get a therapeutic effect.

My earliest recollection of my Aunt's work was in 1935 when, during the summer, she lived at Conesus Lake, one of the Finger Lakes in Upper New York State. She expanded her research by giving treatments to the residents of this small village. I particularly remember those treatments that year because it was the first time I ever found relief from my annual bouts with asthma and hay fever. She would eagerly practice her theories on my feet while explaining the reflex theory as she worked. I must confess that to a youth who was wheezing and sneezing, theory took second place to the blessed relief she was able to give me. Interestingly enough, it was while treating me she convinced herself that in less serious cases, only a few treatments a week sufficed to help most of her patients.

From this small beginning at Conesus Lake, she was so convinced of the value of these treatments that she was determined to write a book, as well as attend all of the health seminars held throughout the country. She did so with the blessing of Dr. Riley who was now convinced that there was something beneficial in Reflexology.

In 1938, she compiled all of her experiences and convictions into a book which she entitled *Stories the Feet Can Tell*. This book did more to help her spread the benefits of Reflexology than any other method she knew. She soon found herself on the program at many health seminars. Her sequel, *Stories the Feet Have Told*, was equally as popular.

Among my aunt's many letters are correspondence with physicians and also medical universities, many asking for more information on her system, others asking her to lecture either at a seminar or in the classroom.

As I have previously mentioned, the initial memories of my Aunt include her working on my feet for asthma and hay fever. Later, I assisted her as she held her seminars and there was a certain fascination for me as I watched people avidly intent on learning this new science to ease pain and to aid the body in controlling diseases. It brought back the memories of my own pleasant relief from those afflictions which struck me every summer and I became convinced that there was a great deal yet to be explored in Reflexology.

After serving a two-year term in the Army Medical Corps, I once again resided with my aunt. I was particularly impressed with her new determination to take her findings and results to every part of the country. This determination became a reality through the late 1940's and during the decade of the 1950's. It was during these later years that she entrusted me with the responsibility of teaching with her at seminars.

But the scope of this activity widened to such an extent that, in 1961, it reached a point when my sister, Eusebia Messenger, R.N., and I found it necessary to assist her on a full time basis. Seven years later the two of us became wholly responsible for continuing her teaching until the mid-1970's when my sister retired. I have continued, along with my wife, Nancy, in the development and teaching of the Ingham Method™ of Reflexology since that time. Of course, all of this work has been accomplished through the *National Institute of Reflexology* ® and the *International Institute of Reflexology* ®.

In December, 1974, Eunice Ingham passed to her eternal reward at the age of 85, after a life dedicated to aiding mankind and thoroughly convinced that Reflexology could aid in easing suffering. She was on the road with that message until the age of 80.

To protect her teachings as well as her original writings, we formed the *National Institute of Reflexology* ® and, shortly after, the *International Institute of Reflexology* ® dedicated to teaching the *Ingham Method* ® of Reflexology throughout the world. Since that time, we have held seminars and named regional directors in all sections of the country and in many parts of the world. Her work and her methods have been copied by some, but the dedication to her original method lives on in the work of our Institute today.

At the present time, her books are still being published and read in seven languages throughout the world.

A fitting tribute to a dedicated woman!

International Institute of Reflexology®
presents
The Ingham Method® Workshops

Theory, Demonstration and Instruction based on over 65 years of research and teaching are combined in a complete workshop to give you the best possible instruction in the art of Reflexology.

These workshops are taught with a combination of multi-media training aids ranging from film graphics to individualized physical application, in order to give you a firm preliminary foundation in Reflexology techniques.

Only our **highly trained professional instructors** are authorized to **teach The Ingham Method**® of Reflexology. If you have any questions regarding our Instructors, please call the I.I.R. at (727) 343-4811.

Learn More Through The Workshops Presented Annually in the United States, Canada, Great Britain, Europe and Australia

---

For more information on our Books, Charts and Workshops contact our Website at: **www.reflexology-usa. net**

PLACE
STAMP
HERE

International Institute of Reflexology®
PO Box 12642
St. Petersburg, Florida 33733-2642
U.S.A.

Ingham Publishing Inc.
Publisher of Books and Charts
on The Ingham Method®

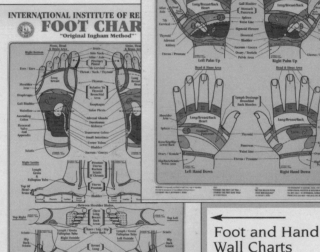

WHAT IS REFLEXOLOGY?

"For the body does not consist of one member but of many. If the foot should say, 'Because I am not a hand, I do not belong to the body,' that would not make it any less a part of the body. And if the ear should say, 'Because I am not the eye, I do not belong to the body,' that would not make it any less a part of the body. If the whole body were an eye, where would be the hearing? If the whole body were an ear, where would be the sense of smell? But as it is, God arranged the organs in the body, each one of them, as he chose. If all were a single organ, where would the body be? As it is, there are many parts, yet one body. The eye cannot say to the hand, 'I have no need of you,' nor again the head to the feet, 'I have no need of you.' If one member suffers, all suffer together. If one member is honored, all rejoice together."

I Corinthians 12:14-21, 26 R.S.V.

WHAT IS REFLEXOLOGY?

THE ART OF FINE TUNING

The more I study and lecture on Reflexology, the more I am amazed at this wonderful structure we walk around in. The human body is a delicately balanced machine that is synergetic . . . everything working together for the benefit of all. I sometimes compare it to a racing machine which works best when it is *in tune* . . . each part functioning at its peak . . . all parts working in harmony to make the machine work at optimum capability.

Now, when the human body is working like that, we call this balanced activity *homeostasis*. Don't let the word frighten you, it is from the Greek language and can be translated as *a state of equilibrium*, or *balance*. I will be using the word here and there throughout this book in reference to our bodily activities.

Perhaps homeostasis can be explained by comparing it to our first example above . . . a racing machine.

Have you ever watched a mechanic fine tune a superb racing machine? He works on each part, constantly adjusting, turning a screw here, twisting a knob there . . . until he is fully satisfied that the machine is in perfect running order so that it will get the maximum response and put out maximum energy. A good mechanic will constantly keep that engine in shape, working even harder when something is slightly amiss. There is a good reason for this . . . he knows that even the slightest component of an engine has to work as well, and as hard, as the largest part. And, if it doesn't . . . then the whole engine is out of tune . . . it will not be working at maximum efficiency.

Now, let's compare the analogy to your own body. As I stated before, your body is a finely tuned wonder. The healthy human body is an amazing machine with everything working in perfect order, the balance being maintained through a system of glands, organs, nerves, chemicals, etc. But let one of these components get out of order, and the effect is felt throughout the entire body system. You are out of *tune*.

And that is the basis for Reflexology.

The principles of Reflexology embody the techniques designed to keep the body's systems operating at peak efficiency . . . or keeping your body *tuned up*.

How?

Well, let's look at my definition of Reflexology.

THE DEFINITION OF REFLEXOLOGY

Reflexology is a science that deals with the principle that there are reflex areas in the feet and hands that correspond to all of the glands, organs and parts of the body. Reflexology is a unique method of using the thumb and fingers on these reflex areas.

Reflexology includes, but is not limited to:

(1) relieve stress and tension;

(2) improve blood supply and promote the unblocking of nerve impulses;

(3) help nature achieve homeostasis.

REFLEXOLOGY RELAXES TENSION

Since approximately 75% of today's diseases are attributable to stress and tension, various body systems are affected in different ways and to varying degrees. One person may exhibit cardiovascular problems, another gastrointestinal upset, anorexia, palpitations, sweating, headaches . . . to mention but a few of the myriad of bodily reactions to stress. Often in my seminars I describe tension as a tourniquet around the body's system . . . a tightening that can lead to serious consequences. I will be discussing stress and tension in much more detail later in this book, always emphasizing its debilitating effects.

REFLEXOLOGY IMPROVES NERVE AND BLOOD SUPPLY

In order to keep the body at a normal balance, it is imperative that the blood and nerve supply to every organ and gland be at a maximum. Of course, the organs and glands contribute to the overall well-being of the body . . . each making contributions to maintaining an efficient, fully-operated mechanism, but all receive their *instructions* from the most intricate of all networks, the nerves.

These cord-like structures, comprised of a collection of nerve fibers, convey impulses between a part of the central nervous system and other regions of the body. They are the *wiring system* of the *house* you call your body. As with any complex wiring system, a *short circuit* can mean trouble.

A short circuit is often caused by tension putting pressure on a vital nerve plexus or even a single nerve structure supplying a vital organ.

As tension is eased, pressure on the nerves and vessels is relaxed, thus improving the flow of blood and its oxygen-rich nutrients to all parts of the body.

REFLEXOLOGY HELPS NATURE ACHIEVE HOMEOSTASIS

Overactive glands or organs can be helped to return to normal. Conversely, if an organ or a gland is underactive, Reflexology can help return it to its normally functioning level. It is important to note here that the normalization action of Reflexology is never one of opposite extreme. In other words, once homeostasis or a normal condition is achieved, it cannot be *unbalanced* by working the area too much. Overworking can cause some minor reactions such as diarrhea or perhaps some nasal mucus being secreted (runny nose). These reactions though are cleansing poisons from the body. Succinctly, Reflexology cannot harm a system, it simply brings it back into balance.

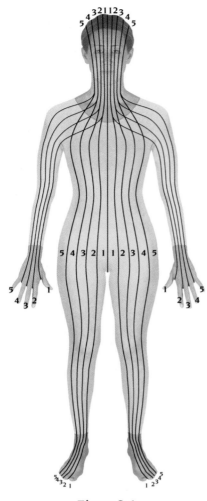

Figure 2.1
10 longitudinal zones of the body

NOTE: Before we continue, let me just insert a word of warning. Unless you are a licensed physician, you should never:

• Diagnose: name a disease

• Prescribe: never prescribe anything nor adjust the client's medication

• Treat for a specific condition

THE ZONE THEORY

As I have previously mentioned, Reflexology embodies the relationship of the reflexes in the feet to all of the glands and organs in the body. Let's now discuss that relationship. Just how does one small area of the foot affect something like the pituitary gland?

Just what is the *link*?

This is where the ZONE THEORY becomes significantly important to every Reflexologist.   To repeat my analogy: the zones are like the wiring in a house, the reflexes travel through the zones similar to electricity through the wires. But please note that this analogy is not to be confused with the nervous system in the body . . . *reflexes* as far as we know today, are **not** nerves.

The link from the feet to the organs and the glands in the body is a series of imaginary longitudinal lines each encompassing a zone. In order to locate the zones accurately in the arms and hands, the thumbs need to be placed towards the body, the opposite of the anatomical position. (**See Figure 2.1**)

The word *zone* is used for several significant reasons . . . but first, let's take a closer look at just what constitutes the zone theory.

There are ten (10) lines or *zones*. Easy enough to remember: one for each finger and one for each toe. Zone one (1) starts at the thumb and great toe.

As the illustration shows, these zones run the entire length of the body . . . from the top of the head to the tips of the toes. (**See Figure 2.1**)

It is extremely important that Reflexologists become *zone oriented*, so they must be thoroughly familiar with the basic zones and the anatomy associated within them.

Let's present another analogy which will serve to give you a better and clearer understanding of the zone theory.

Let's bake a fruit cake in the shape of a gingerbread man. And then fill it with all of those things one generally finds in such a con-coction . . . fruits and nuts and bits of spices and whatever else the cook decides to throw in. Now, when our little man is finally done, we are going to take him and cut ten longitudinal slices . . . from top to bottom. (**See Figure 2.2**) Each of these longitudinal slices represents a zone. Everything within that slice (zone) belongs to that zone . . . from head to toe and from front to back.

Got the picture?

Look at the illustration again. Now, take a good look at your own body. Think of your body marked with these ten zones. Start with the small toe, that is a zone. Notice how that zone extends from the small toe right on up to the top of your head. Next, look carefully at the great toe. There are five (5) zones in the great toe since it represents one-half of the head. Now, imagine that you are going to remove one of those longitudinal slices from your own body. Which organs are going to be included within that slice?

To help you answer that question, take a look at the basic anatomy charts. (**See Figure 2.3**) Imagine that same zone line running from the toes to the head . . . line one (1) to five (5) on the left, and corresponding lines one (1) to five (5) on the right. Become acquainted with drawing those zone lines over that basic anato-my and your task as a Reflexologist is going to be much easier.

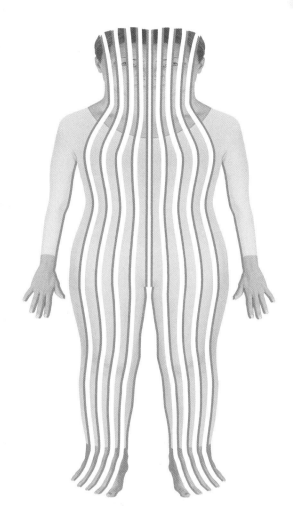

Figure 2.2
10 longitudinal zones of the body

And remember: An organ or a gland found in a specific zone will have its reflex in the corresponding zone of the foot.

Any sensitivity located in a specific area on the foot will signal to you that there could be congestion in that area.

The importance of this fact can be made even clearer if you return to the basic anatomy chart and run your zone lines over it again. Notice that by working an area of the foot, you are affecting glands and organs within that zone . . . that *slice* of the gin-gerbread man.

It should become evident then, that by working the entire foot, you are affecting the entire side of the body; the right foot representing the right half of the body, the left foot representing the left half of the body. While we are on that subject, it is important to remember another significant aspect of Reflexology: an abnormality in **any** part of the zone **may** affect anything in that zone.

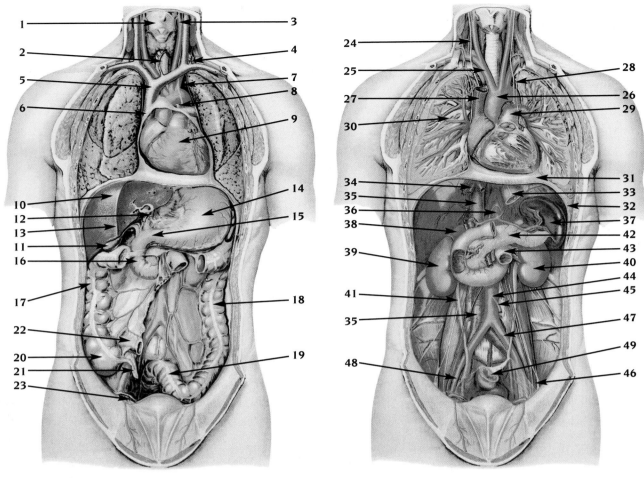

Figure 2.3
Anatomical chart

1. Thyroid cartilage (Cartilago thyreoidea)
2. Windpipe (Trachea)
3. Left common carotid
   (A. carotis communis sinistra)
4. Thoracic duct (Ductus thoract . cus,
5. Superior cava (V cava superior)
6. Pericardium (Pericardium)
7. Phrenic (N. phrenicus)
8. Vagus (N. vagus)
9. Heart (Cor)
10. Liver (Hepar)
11. Gall bladder (Vlessicafellea)
12. Hepatic artery, portal vein, hepatic duct
   (A. hepatica propria, V. Portae, ductus hepaticus)
13. Foramen of Winslow (Foramen epiploicum)
14. Stomach (Ventriculus)
15. Pylorus (Pylorus)
16. Duodenum (Duodenum)
17. Ascending colon (Colon ascendens)
18. Descending colon (Colon descendens)
19. Sigmoid (Colon sigmoideum)
20. Blind intestine (Caecum)
21. Appendix (Processus vermiformis)
22. Ileum (Ileum)
23. Spermatic duct (Ductus deferens)
24. Vertebral (A. vertebralis)
25. Brachiocephalic (A. bracbiocephalica)

26. Aortic arch (Arcus aortae)
27. Superior cava (V. cava superior)
28. Left vagus (N. vagus sinister)
29. Pulmonary (A. pulmonalis)
30. Pulmonary vessels and bronchii
   (Vasa pulmonalia et broncbii
31. Pleura (Pleura)
32. Diaphragm (Diaphragma)
33. Cardiac end of stomach (Cardia)
34. Hepatic veins (Vt,. hepaticae)
35. Inferior cava (V. cava inferior)
36. Celiac (Truncus coeliacus
37. Spleen and splenic vessels Anatomical Cbarts
   Used By Permiss (Lien et vasa lienalia)
38. Right suprarenal gland
   (Glandula suprarenalis dextra)
39. Right kidney (Ren dexter)
40. Left kidney (Ren sinister)
41. Ureter (Ureter)
42. Pancreas (Pancreas)
43. Duodenojejunal flexure
   (Flexura duodenojejunalis)
44. Abdominal aorta (Aorta abdominalis)
45. Inferior mesenteric (A. mesenterica inferior)
46. Femoral nerve (N. femoralis)
47. Common iliac (A. et V. iliaca communis)
48. External iliac (A. et V. iliaca external)
49. Rectum (Rectum)

LET'S GET ORIENTED

In order to aid you in visualizing the significant relationship between the feet and the entire body in perspective, carefully study **Figure 2.4**. Note the similarities of the feet to the entire body.

To become acquainted with some standard reference terms we are going to be using in this book, look down at your own feet as you stand on them.

Take a good look because we will be defining the **medial** side (inside) as the great toe side . . . and the **lateral** side (outside) as the small toe side.

You are standing on the **plantar** surface (bottom) of your feet, and as you look down, you are looking at the **dorsal** surface (top) of your feet. As you look at your toes, you can bend down and touch the tips of the toes – **distal**. The back of the foot is the heel – **proximal**.

Remembering these reference terms is as easy as standing on your own two feet.

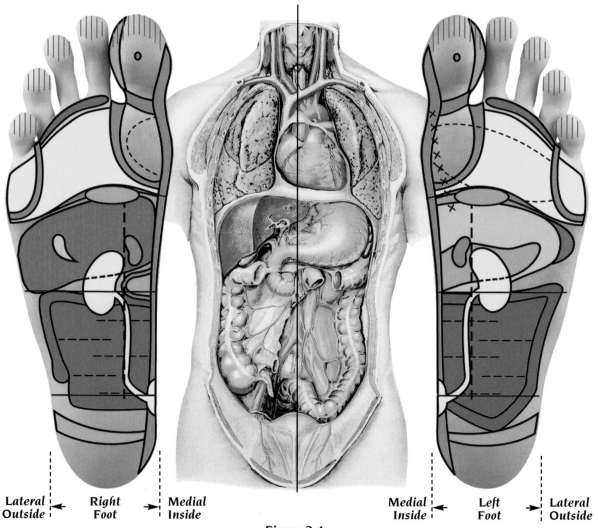

| Lateral | | Right | | Medial | | Medial | | Left | | Lateral |
| Outside | | Foot | | Inside | | Inside | | Foot | | Outside |

Figure 2.4
The relationship between the reflexes of the feet and the body
Anatomical Charts Used By Permission NYSTROM, Division of Carnation

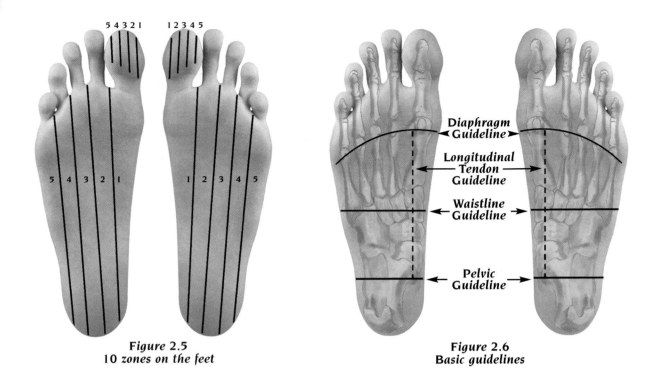

Figure 2.5
10 *zones on the feet*

Figure 2.6
Basic guidelines

While we are talking about toes, remember the great toe contains **all five zones** of the head. The great toe is your general orientation to the head area.

This is not to say that the other toes are unimportant; indeed, they are invaluable for **fine tuning** those zones of the head applicable to each toe. (**See Figure 2.5**) Each toe, of course, delineating its own specific head and neck region.

While we are becoming oriented with the feet/body relationship there is something which we have not yet discussed. There is an aspect of Reflexology everyone should become thoroughly familiar with: **Body Relation Guidelines**.

There are guidelines running either horizontally across the foot or vertically up and down the foot. These are a natural phenomenon since they represent the all important *plexus* areas and are areas within the body where constant multiple activities are happening; where nerves, important organs and glands are located.

There are four major guidelines which you should become familiar with: (**See Figure 2.6**)

- The Diaphragm Guideline

- The Waistline Guideline

- The Pelvic Guideline

- The Longitudinal Tendon Guideline or Tendon Guideline

These guidelines are important landmarks which we will be discussing later. Another landmark you should become familiar with includes the metatarsal or *ball* of the foot.

Meanwhile, back to our illustration. As you take a good look, one important thing to remember is our analogy of the zone *slice*. The zone areas of the feet are no different. Remember, you are looking at the two feet as if you were looking at our gingerbread man. **The zones go all the way through the feet.** If you can visualize the human body superimposed on the plantar surface of the feet, you are on your way to understanding the science of Reflexology. (**See Figure 2.4**)

Let's continue with that visualization.

I have already discussed the head as represented by the great toe and the smaller toes. Now, let's look at another of the more important areas of the human body and, incidentally, one which causes more trouble . . . the spine. We will be discussing the spine in another section of this book; right now, we are locating the spinal zone (Zone One).

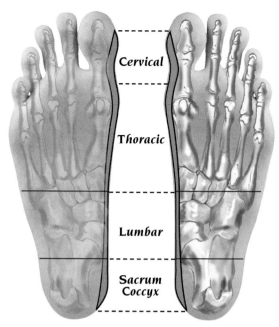

Figure 2.7
Spinal reflex

The spine, of course, helps to hold the head, therefore, it will be the center or dividing line of the body. But, what about the fact that the right foot represents the right half of the body while the left foot represents the left half?

The answer to that can be seen in **Figure 2.7**. Note that each foot has a spinal reflex area and it is located along the medial edge of each foot.

Anatomically, of course, the shoulder area is beneath the head and neck, consequently the very base of the toes would represent the reflex to some of the shoulder muscles.

One of the more important guidelines runs horizontally across the body, and so it is reflected in a lateral line across the feet. This line is termed the diaphragm guideline. Associated with the diaphragm is the solar plexus, somewhat like a *nerve switchboard*, which makes all kinds of connections to various parts of the body . . . a good reason to become thoroughly familiar with this reflex area.

The solar plexus is located in the body just at the base of the body's breastbone or *sternum*. Immediately below that is a large muscular band, shaped like the top of an opened umbrella. This band, the diaphragm, separates the interior body cavity. If we were to take a closer look at the area below the diaphragm, we would see the liver, the stomach and also the gathering or *crossing* (plexus) of many important nerves.

The diaphragm/solar plexus reflex on the feet is found just below the metatarsal pad or ball of each foot. When the toes are flexed back, the foot looks like it is *sticking its chest out* . . . right below that *chest* is the line you are looking for. The chest area is usually easy to find since, in most persons, the area is delineated by a darker color.

Now, let's take a look at the second guideline . . . the waistline guideline, another lateral line. This one is a cinch!

If you run your fingers down the lateral side of the foot, about halfway down, your fingers will feel a *high spot*. This high spot, or protuberance, is formed by the head of the fifth metatarsal bone. When you locate the high spot and draw a lateral line across each foot, you have the waistline guideline . . . a dividing *belt line* that makes it easier to locate the reflexes for the various organs and glands that are found either above, below or on the waistline guideline.

Another important guideline which nature easily points out for you is the pelvic guideline. This guideline is found at the beginning of the heel where there is a noticeable color and texture change. This is one of the areas of the foot where the thick, callused skin often makes working so difficult that special techniques are required. But that is not to detract from the fact that it is a very important area to the Reflexologist, since it is the reflex area for the lower back, the sigmoid colon and associative nerves.

The final important guideline is the longitudinal tendon guideline. This guideline is located between the great toe and the second toe and is found by extending the great toe back. This action causes the longitudinal tendon on the plantar surface of the foot to become more pronounced. It is easily located by gently running the thumb or finger over the plantar surface of the foot . . . the cord-like tendon will feel like a taut band. If pushing on the band causes the great toe to *nod its head*, you have found the tendon.

For clarity, why not take another look at the *anatomy chart*, in order to become familiar with these main divisions and the basic glands and organs within each division and then visualize them on the feet.

While you are studying the chart, take a closer look at the groin area. This curved area has special significance when we locate it on the feet since it rounds out to include the ankle. (**See Figure 2.8**) The groin area is found where the leg is joined to the body; the groin reflex is located where the foot is joined to the ankle.

Figure 2.8
Groin reflex

ORGANS . . . THE INSIDE STORY

Like a suitcase packed with the necessities for travel, the body is also packed with vital organs and glands in somewhat the same manner. Everything packed on top of everything else.

Once again, a glance at our anatomy chart will confirm this fact.   Start at the spine, the midline of the body, as a means of orienting yourself to the relationship between the foot reflex points and the organs of the body. Now, you have a reference point for each foot. Then use the waistline guideline for your horizontal or lateral marker. The most important body organs are located in four distinct quadrants. Now, transfer that picture of the feet keeping one important fact in mind: some of those organs will extend over into another quadrant. So you must work both reflex areas to be sure to cover the entire organ's reflex. Want an example? Study the heart. See how it extends over the midline area? What zones would you work to completely cover the heart area?

Once again . . . remember that the feet are a *reflection* of the body with all its glands, nerves and organs having distinct locations on the feet. Being sure that you are thoroughly familiar with this concept of location, makes the zone theory so much easier.

REFERRAL AREAS

The referral areas are an interesting and extremely useful adjunct to Reflexology. They allow you to *refer* one area of the body to an alternate area, i.e., arm to leg, leg to arm, etc.

The right and left hand are referral areas for the right and left foot respectively. To fully grasp this concept study **Figures 2.9, 2.10**. Note that the palm of the hand is facing forward (supine) i.e., in the anatomical position. So this will make the arm bend in the opposite direction from the leg. This will orient you to the anatomical relationships.

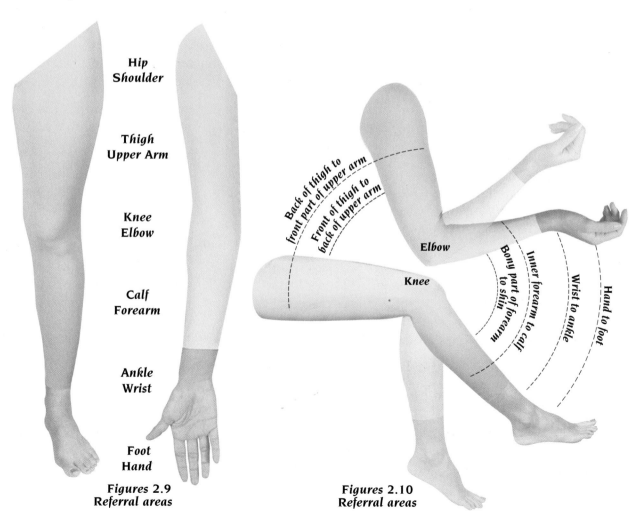

Hip
Shoulder

Thigh
Upper Arm

Knee
Elbow

Calf
Forearm

Ankle
Wrist

Foot
Hand

Figures 2.9
Referral areas

Back of thigh to front part of upper arm

Front of thigh to back of upper arm

Elbow

Knee

Bony part of forearm to shin

Inner forearm to calf

Wrist to ankle

Hand to foot

Figures 2.10
Referral areas

- The palm of the hand refers to the plantar surface of the foot

- The inner forearm refers to the calf of the leg

- The bony part of the forearm refers to the shin bone

- The elbow refers to the kneecap

- The front of the elbow refers to the back of the knee

- The front of the upper arm refers to the back of the thigh

- The back of the upper arm refers to the front of the thigh

Also, note the relationship of the thumb to the great toe . . . the thumb being in the opposite position to the great toe.

The basic reason we call these areas *referrals* is simply because of the anatomical relationship existing between them.

For instance, it is quite easy to see the similarity of the ankle to the wrist if we were like other animals and walked on *all fours*. The articulated movement of the ankle would correspond to that of the wrist for motion.

Now, suppose there were a misstep and an ankle became badly sprained. As a Reflexologist, we would know that pressure would soon build up in the area of the sprain unless immediately relieved. Naturally, the ankle is too injured to touch, much less work, so we would work on the wrist . . . for it is anatomically related to the ankle . . . a logical choice to prevent soreness, swelling or other possible complications.

To repeat, a referral area is an anatomically related area which can be worked instead of, or in addition to, the affected area. This is true of **all** referral areas.

One way to remember: when thinking of the ankle, refer to the wrist; when thinking of the elbow, refer to the knee, etc. Your client can be taught to use the referral areas and also how to work on their hands between follow-up sessions. This exercise will reinforce your own efforts.

And why is all of this so significant?

For the simple reason that if you can't work an area on the foot, you can work the corresponding area on the hand, or the elbow, etc. When there is a severe injury, say a broken leg, you then simply select the corresponding area on the arm and work that area in order to help the circulation to the injured area and ultimately hasten the healing process. The basic reason the Reflexologist uses the foot is simply because it is one of the most pampered and protected areas of the body and, so is one of the most sensitive to touch. Also, the foot's resemblance to the body's outline makes it easy to visualize the body on the foot.

HELPER AREAS

Helper areas are additional areas worked to aid the specific area of congestion. They are the *reinforcements* you send to aid the specific area.

For instance: a headache. You would naturally work the great toe which represents the head. To help that area, we would also work the neck, seventh (7th) cervical and coccyx reflexes as this may be the area causing the headache. A headache is usually telling us that there is an imbalance somewhere in the body.

Helper areas are just that . . . they are areas that when worked, help to relieve tension or congestion associated with the afflicted area. They are reflexes that may have a **direct or indirect effect** on the **afflicted area** and are the *reinforcements* needed to make sure you reach the desired results. You are sending **help** to the afflicted area.

Chapter 3

COMMON TERMS DEFINED

"Nature does nothing in vain."

Aristotle

COMMON TERMS DEFINED

MEDIAL SIDE OF THE FOOT
The medial side of the foot will be defined as the great toe side or the inside of the foot.

LATERAL SIDE OF THE FOOT
The lateral side of the foot will be defined as the little toe side or the outside of the foot.

DORSAL SURFACE or DORSUM OF THE FOOT
The dorsal surface of the foot will be defined as the top of the foot.

PLANTAR SURFACE OF THE FOOT
The plantar surface of the foot will be defined as the bottom or sole of the foot.

DISTAL PART OF THE FOOT
The distal part of the foot is the part farthest away from the body, e.g. the toes.

PROXIMAL PART OF THE FOOT
The proximal part of the foot is the part nearest the body, e.g. the heel.

BASIC THUMB TECHNIQUE
The basic thumb technique is executed by bending the first joint at a 45° angle while using the **medial edge** of the thumb.

BASIC FINGER TECHNIQUE
The basic finger technique is executed by working with the **medial edge** of the finger, in conjunction with bending the **first joint** of that finger.

BASIC HOLDING TECHNIQUE
The basic holding technique is executed by placing the heel of the hand on the ball (metatarsal pad) of the foot with the fingers relaxed over the toes. Push the foot **back** and **drop the wrist**. It is very important to drop the wrist because this action relaxes the longitudinal tendon.

LEVERAGE
Leverage is obtained by the use of the fingers in opposition to the working thumb or when you are working with the fingers, the leverage will be made with the thumb in opposition to the fingers. The leverage gives the thumb or fingers the strength and endurance for smooth walking.

RELAXING TECHNIQUES
These are special techniques that feel very good and are designed to promote relaxation. These techniques are also used for working the relative reflex area to help improve the circulation.

PIN-POINT TECHNIQUE

The "Pin-point" technique is used when working a very small and exact reflex area, such as the pituitary gland or the sigmoid flexure. These are areas that have to be contacted with great accuracy in order to be effective.

HOOK-IN, BACK-UP TECHNIQUE

The "Hook-in, Back-up" technique is used when a reflex area needs to be pin-pointed such as the pituitary gland, ileocecal valve, and the sigmoid flexure reflexes. The medial corner of the thumb is placed on the specific reflex and, instead of walking the thumb, it is pushed in and the thumb is pulled back toward the hand, then the wrist is dropped. This is a steady motion where the thumb is *planted* with pressure and moves slightly back towards your hand.

DIAPHRAGM GUIDELINE

The diaphragm is a thin muscle forming the floor of the chest at the base of the lungs and forms the roof of the abdominal cavity. The guideline to the diaphragm will be found at the base of the distal metatarsal heads where the skin color and texture changes.

WAISTLINE GUIDELINE

The waistline guideline is found by locating the high spot on the lateral side of the foot about halfway down. This high spot is the protrusion of the head of the fifth metatarsal bone. After finding this high spot, draw an imaginary line across the foot; this will be the waistline guideline.

LONGITUDINAL TENDON GUIDELINE

The longitudinal tendon guideline is found on the plantar surface of the foot when the great toe is extended back. The longitudinal tendon (*between the diaphragm guideline and the pelvic guideline*) will protrude and feel like a taut band.

PELVIC GUIDELINE

The pelvic guideline is located on the medial side, at the end of the soft arch area where the heel starts. The heel itself is often darker in color and of a heavier texture. The guideline is where these two areas meet. Draw an imaginary line across the foot, this will be the pelvic guideline.

WALKING THE RIDGE

"Walking the Ridge" refers to where the base of the toes join onto the foot and is used when working the eye and ear reflexes.

CRISS-CROSS MOTION

The "Criss-Cross Motion" is obtained by working an area in several directions, first with one hand and then with the alternate hand. Usually, you will be working at an angle across the foot from the medial to the lateral side and then from the lateral to the medial side. The reason for working in this manner is to be sure you cover the whole area thoroughly. Sometimes there will be more sensitivity from one direction than from another.

CUBOID NOTCH

The cuboid notch is found as you run your thumb or finger down the lateral side of the foot until you reach the low spot. This soft, hollow area below the waistline guideline of the foot will be the cuboid notch.

GRITTY REFLEXES

Grittiness is found in the feet when you are working some of the reflexes, i.e., the neck and shoulder reflexes. They will feel like little grains of salt under your fingers or thumbs. You will have to develop some sensitivity with your fingers and thumbs in order to recognize them. Gritty reflexes are not found in all areas of the foot.

TENDER AREAS

Tender areas are reflex areas that feel tight or grainy under your thumb and may provide the client with some discomfort when pressure is applied to this area. You can sometimes tell when you have reached a tender spot as the person tenses up or winces. Watching the client's face can tell you when to lighten your pressure.

SOLAR PLEXUS

The solar plexus is also known as our *abdominal brain* because it contains so many nerves and nerve networks. It is located at the end of the sternum and in the diaphragm. It is part of the nervous system and it relays its messages through the diaphragm. On the foot, the solar plexus reflex is located on the diaphragm guideline between the great toe and the second toe.

7th CERVICAL REFLEX

The 7th Cervical reflex is found at the base of the great toe on the medial edge where the great toe is joined onto the foot. On the body, the 7th cervical is found on the back of the neck where the spinus process protrudes at the base of the neck.

HIGH SPOT OF THE ANKLEBONE

The high spot of the anklebone will be found on either the medial or lateral side of the ankle at the highest point of the rounded protuberance.

Chapter 4

TECHNIQUES

*"And let the beauty of the Lord our God
be upon us; and establish thou the work of our
hands upon us . . . "*

Psalms 90:17

TECHNIQUES

INTRODUCTION

The Ingham Method ® *of Reflexology* was pioneered, researched and developed in the early 1930's by the late Eunice Ingham and is the leading method of Reflexology in use today throughout the world. Applied Reflexology techniques are different from any other form of contact therapy. It is this difference that makes Reflexology so unique. The explanations and diagrams set up here should be diligently studied and adhered to, remembering that *perfect practice makes perfect.* Without this perfect practice, the all important sensitivity of touch will not be achieved.

As an orthodox Reflexologist, you will use no instruments, oils or creams as you work the feet; rather, you will develop a keen sense of touch using the tactile senses of the fingers and the thumb. Corn starch is preferred if your hands or the client's feet are damp.

You can read and study, but practical learning is a **must** to achieve the best results. The *International Institute of Reflexology* ® was developed to bring this practical hands-on training to you.

Another thing you will learn is to always keep your fingernails trimmed to an acceptable length so they cannot scratch or dig into the feet.

And while on the subject of practical applications, I have found that a recliner-type chair provides the best working arrangement for your client and a secretarial-type chair for the practitioner, since the height is adjustable and the wheels on the chair allow you to move more easily into various working positions. It is also important to be able to rest your back against the back of the chair to prevent bad posture and unnecessary fatigue.

BASIC TECHNIQUES

The Reflexologist develops an efficient sensitivity and the ability to conserve energy by using less effort in working the reflex areas through the use of the following working techniques. A good Reflexologist learns through the sense of touch, as well as a developed sense of observation, both of which are fundamental to this science.

In order to accomplish this, we will be discussing the following techniques:

- Basic holding technique.

- Basic thumb technique.

- Leverage.

- Basic finger technique.

- Hook-in, back-up technique.

- Pivot-point technique.

We are going to discuss each one of these techniques and their application as we go from the basic to the well-defined *pin-point* technology. But first, we are going to consider the fact that no matter how well we develop these working techniques, we cannot really accomplish our goal unless we learn one other basic and elementary principle of Reflexology . . . the proper holding techniques. There are many reasons for the various configurations for holding the feet properly, and they will be discussed as we develop each of the techniques. The procedures being described here are all depicted as I would work on a client . . . their right foot will be on my left, and vice versa. For simplicity all techniques will be demonstrated on the **right foot** unless otherwise stated.

Since Reflexology works with both feet and since the reflex areas can be worked with both hands, the hand which will be working the reflex areas will now be termed the **working** hand. The other hand which naturally works as an adjunctive to the working hand, will be called the **holding** hand.

Each of these techniques we will be describing has its own holding as well as working techniques, so it is important for the trained Reflexologist not only to develop the working techniques, but also to become familiar with the adjunctive holding techniques which allows them to acquire a cooperative effect and thus a more successful application of Reflexology. Remember it this way: to successfully work the feet, we need teamwork with the hands.

BASIC HOLDING TECHNIQUE

The heel of the holding hand will be placed firmly on the metatarsal pad of the foot with the fingers relaxed over the toes and the thumb on the medial edge of the great toe or the small toe, depending on which hand you are using. **Drop** the wrist slightly to relax the longitudinal tendon of the foot. This gives you control over the foot and allows you to push the foot back or to bring it forward using the natural spring of the ankle joint. This specific hold will be used for the majority of the techniques utilized on the bottom (plantar surface) of the foot. (**See Figure 4.1**)

BASIC THUMB TECHNIQUE

For the beginner, the thumb technique is a very basic one and can be demonstrated by placing the palm of the hand down on a table. (**See Figure 4.2**) You will notice the natural position of your hand on the table and partic-

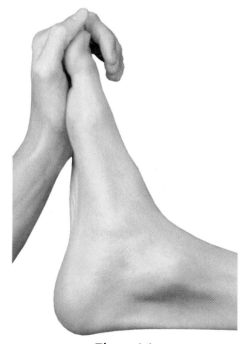

Figure 4.1
Basic holding technique

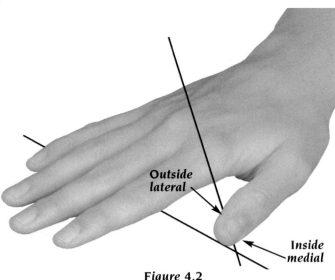

Outside
lateral

Inside
medial

Figure 4.2
Position for the basic thumb technique

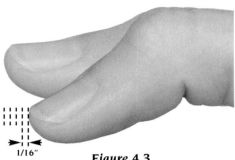

1/16"

Figure 4.3
Basic thumb walking technique

ularly the angle of the thumb where it rests on the table, this is going to be the **working area** of the thumb. The inside (medial) edge of the thumb makes contact with the table. This is the part of the thumb that you should be using.

You will notice that your thumb is at a natural 45° angle. Now that you have become familiar with the working edge of the thumb, let's *walk* the thumb; it's the secret of using the thumb technique successfully. But before walking the thumb, let's learn the secret of a successful walk: the bending of the 1st joint of the thumb. You can demonstrate this to yourself by holding your thumb below the 1st joint and then bending the top joint. That's the important action you will be using.

Now, taking away your hand from the 1st joint of the thumb, try to make the thumb bend as before. Place the hand back on the table with the thumb in the natural position and with a steady, even pressure, walk the thumb by slightly bending and unbending the 1st joint . . . it will "creep" forward in this natural position. We advise against straightening the thumb all the way for it allows too much flat thumb surface to come in contact with the foot thus missing the critical reflexes. (**See Figure 4.3**)

While using the thumb walking technique, you will be combining it with an equally important and naturally acquired technique called **leverage**. An important fact to remember is that leverage can be obtained by using firm, even pressure with the 4 fingers of the working hand in opposition to the thumb. The foot is between the thumb and the 4 fingers.

LEVERAGE

As an example of leverage, place your right thumb on your left forearm and do the walking motion without letting the fingers touch the arm. Now, place the fingers of your working hand firmly underneath the arm for leverage in opposition to your thumb and do the walking motion with your thumb, letting the fingers follow along as you move.

Notice how much more pressure you have. This is leverage!

Now that we have discussed the basic thumb technique and the necessary leverage, let's walk the thumb. Remember, we want to walk the thumb by bending and straightening the 1st joint and taking tiny bites. It is necessary when learning this technique to practice, practice, practice until you feel an **even steady pressure**. This is not an intermittent pressure, but a steady pressure as the thumb bends like a snail who leaves a steady, even trail. The thumb should never become concave as it walks forward.

Let's practice walking the thumb on an area of the foot. It is best to practice the thumb technique by working the center of the foot that is soft and pliant and doesn't require a lot of pressure. This also gives you an opportunity to learn the general holding technique in this area. Remember, the holding hand is going to be used to hold the foot in a suitable position to *control* it. In this instance, place the heel of your hand on the ball of the foot, with fingers relaxed over the toes. Push the foot back and drop the wrist. (**See Figure 4.4**) This opens up the area and allows the thumb easy access to the reflex area. Now you can practice the thumb technique on the bottom of the foot by applying a constant steady pressure, using the medial corner of the thumb. Another hint for the thumb technique: the thumb always walks forward and never backs up or goes sideways.

While you are practicing walking the thumb in that soft area of the foot, check how much leverage your fingers are providing. You will note as you work the area you must keep your fingers moving forward slowly with the thumb or you lose the leverage. The thumb and fingers must be opposite each other to get maximum leverage. Let the leverage fingers follow along as you work; don't let them get too far away so that the hand is stretched out as it will become fatigued. Be sure not to over stretch your thumb joints as this will eventually cause problems with your hands. To reiterate: **the correct technique protects your hands from damaging incorrect repetitive motions.**

This is the basic thumb technique. On this technique, you will be building your whole career as a Reflexologist. And, as in any science, practice is going to pay off and as you begin to develop your Reflexology techniques you will be able to *concentrate* on the reflex areas so necessary for a successful session.

Another thing you may notice as you begin is that while working or practicing, an area of the thumb or the joint on that thumb may become a little sore. Just as

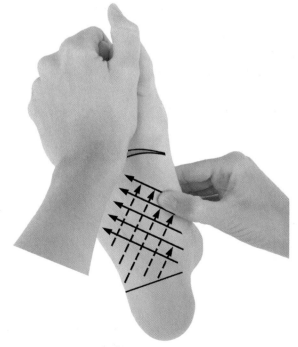

Figure 4.4
Working between the pelvic and diaphragm guidelines

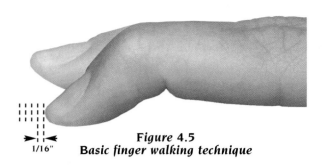

1/16"

Figure 4.5
Basic finger walking technique

in developing any muscle (as any athlete can affirm) it takes time to build strength and it takes a lot of practice. Remember to maintain constant pressure as the thumb walks forward. A good idea would be to test your thumb technique on your arm. The real test is a feeling of constant pressure much as if someone were drawing a line down the arm with a felt tip pen. If this steady pressure is not evident, there is more of a feeling of *on and off* pressure, then review the technique including the bending of that 1st joint.

As you review this technique, keep in mind that you are working on the basic rule to effectively work the reflex areas. You must maintain that steady constant pressure and the necessary leverage. It is the leverage that gives your thumb strength, as well as protect your thumbs against injury, as you work the reflex areas of the foot. The angle that you use aids your total leverage as well.

BASIC FINGER TECHNIQUE

The second technique that a Reflexologist learns is basically the same as the thumb technique, bending only the 1st joint of the fingers.

This time, in the finger technique, leverage is obtained by the thumb when it is in opposition to the fingers.

As in all Reflexology operating modes, the finger technique needs constant practice. The object of that practice is the same as with the thumb technique: taking creeping motions by smaller and smaller **bites** and exerting a constant and steady forward pressure. Once again, we do not want the *on and off* type of pressure. And, as with the thumb, the finger always moves in a forward direction, never backwards or sideways. (**See Figure 4.5**)

It is also important to remember that the index, third and fourth fingers can walk individually or together, however we will be using the index finger for many of these techniques. As the fingers are generally narrower, we use them to work certain areas which could not be worked as effectively by using the thumbs. This also allows our thumbs to **rest** during a session.

Now, of course, one finger cannot walk off by itself without taking the other fingers along, so the other fingers help with the leverage of the index finger. Your first difficulty in executing the finger technique will probably involve bending the first joint of the finger. Practice by holding the index finger just below the 1st joint and then bending the 1st joint only. Other things to avoid as you practice are scratching or digging the fingernail into the skin; sometimes reversing or allowing fingers to draw back and burn the skin rather than a forward constant pressure; some people merely roll the finger from side to side. These difficulties can be overcome only with practice, practice, practice.

Only the 1st joint of the finger or thumb is flexed at an angle of 45° and not 90° for three reasons:

    1. It will cause too much stress on the joint of the person giving the session.

    2. The person receiving session will feel your nails.

    3. You will miss a lot of contact with the skin.

When working an area, you must keep the working finger or thumb parallel to the surface being worked on and at a slight angle taking small *bites*. When working many areas of the foot, such as the spinal and sinus reflexes, the fingers are used to give the working thumb leverage and smoothness throughout the whole operation.

A tender reflex must be worked from several directions: up, down and across. Very often, walking over an area in one direction will not elicit any sensitivity, but coming back in the opposite direction will often be quite sensitive. The reason for this directional response is not exactly understood. It is possible that the subcutaneous granulations that we sometimes feel and work on are laid down in layers. Try to feel any changes in the tissues on which contact is being made, i.e. granulations, changes of tension or a difference in the texture or the feeling of the reflex.

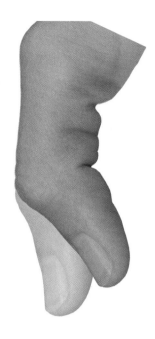

Figure 4.6
Hook-in, back-up technique

"HOOK-IN, BACK-UP" TECHNIQUE or "BUMBLEBEE ACTION"

As you progress through your Reflexology techniques and begin to understand the anatomy associated with working Reflexology, you will soon discover that there are certain target areas that the Reflexologist must work which call for *pin-point* accuracy. When it comes to pin-point accuracy, you will usually use the *hook-in, back-up* technique. I have termed this the *bumblebee* technique. If any of you have been subjected to a sting of that little insect you are probably aware of its habit of implanting the stinger into your anatomy. He lands on your arm and backs up the stinger into your flesh. This is basically the action your thumb is going to use. You're going to hook it in and back it up.

Just as you did using the thumb technique, you must bend the 1st joint of the thumb slightly and exert pressure with the medial (inside) corner of the thumb. Once you have placed the thumb in that position on the reflex point, push in and bend the thumb to approximately a 90° angle as you drop the wrist. Just as that bee lands on a spot and backs that stinger into your flesh, the thumb will emulate the same motion. It will *hook-in and back-up*. (**See Figure 4.6**) Be sure when you use this technique not to slide across the surface of the skin but keep the thumb in contact and only move the underlying tissue.

Since this technique calls for pin-pointing and usually the reflex area represents deep points within the body; leverage is extremely important. For the hook-in, back-up technique, we use the wrist as well as the fingers for leverage.

We use the term pin-pointing since there is no *walking* with the thumb. Place the thumb on a small point, hook-in, back-up by dropping the wrist.

"PIVOT POINT" TECHNIQUE

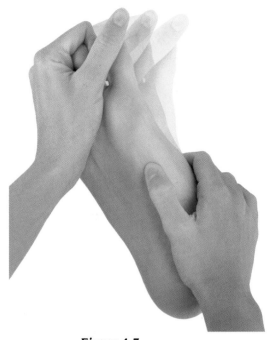

Figure 4.7
Pivot point technique

The pivot point technique is a valuable aid in working particularly tender areas. Once the area is pin-pointed, we're going to put pressure on this area with the thumb. Use the basic holding position with the holding hand and flex the foot slowly onto the thumb. Flex several times; this gives increased pressure at the reflex point. Then slowly shift the thumb around the region, only working to the discomfort tolerance of the person. Watch out for digging in with your fingernail. This technique can be done with either hand and is ideally adapted for use when working on your own feet. (**See Figure 4.7**)

NOTE: Some of the techniques can be administered to your own feet and can be very effective, limited, of course, by your own agility.

DISCOMFORT

Remember that when giving a session, the idea is not to cause unnecessary discomfort. The face of the person receiving treatment must always be observed and the pressure adjusted as necessary. Work for an indicative sign, what a trained Reflexologist calls, *relaxing pain*. Yes, there is such a thing.

RELAXING TECHNIQUES

SIDE-TO-SIDE (Back and Forth)

Place the center of the palms of the hands, one on the medial side on the 1st metatarsal head and one on the lateral side on the 5th metatarsal head, with the fingers relaxed, and then move the hands rapidly back and forth. *The hands will be going in the opposite direction from each other.* Be sure your hands are held firmly against the foot so as not to burn or slide on the skin. (**See Figure 4.8**) If the fingers are relaxed they will allow the outside hand to gently slap the top of the foot, this will add to the relaxing sensation.

METATARSAL KNEADING

Place the fingers of the right hand (holding hand) on the dorsum of the foot from the medial side, with the index finger placed just below the base of the toes and the thumb in a vertical position resting on the medial edge of the foot. This hand should prevent the foot from moving backwards and forwards. With the left hand make a fist with the flat part placed against the plantar surface of the foot (metatarsal area) directly opposite the right hand. First push the fist against the metatarsal pad, then as you knead with the holding hand release a little pressure with the fist. You should feel the metatarsal bones moving in a wavelike motion as you knead with the one hand and slightly relax the pressure with the fist. When using this technique, keep both hands in contact with the foot at all times. When one hand is either pushing or kneading, the other hand is just slightly relaxed. Repeat several times. (**See Figure 4.9**)

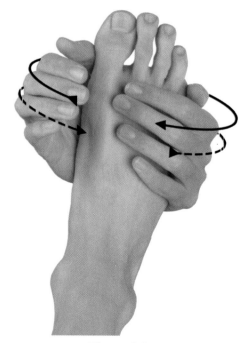

Figure 4.8
Side-to-side relaxation technique

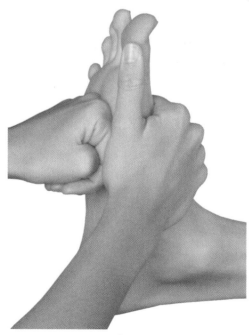

Figure 4.9
Metatarsal kneading relaxation technique

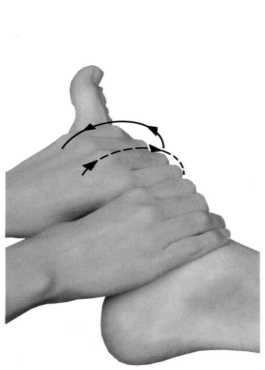

Figure 4.10
Spinal twist relaxation technique

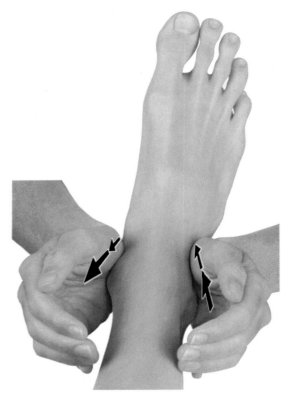

Figure 4.11
Ankle loosening relaxation technique

SPINAL TWIST

Place the hands together with the palms facing down and index fingers touching each other; the thumbs will also be down. With the foot tipped out, place the hands as a unit firmly around the foot, with the webbing between the thumbs and fingers placed on the spinal reflex area and the thumbs on the plantar surface of the foot. The center of the two hands will be placed on or slightly above the pelvic guideline, keeping your arms straight and then **drop** your wrists. The hands should be used as a unit keeping all the fingers together and the hands touching at all times. The hand closest to the heel will remain stationary and firmly support the foot, while the other hand will twist slowly and smoothly back and forth as far as possible in each direction. After several movements, slide the two hands together gradually inching toward the toes and continue the twisting movement remembering to keep the hand toward the heel stationary and firm at all times. Continue this process until the hand nearest the toes is over the great toe. Be sure when you twist the foot that you move the foot evenly and as far as possible in both directions. (**See Figure 4.10**)

ANKLE LOOSENING

Place the heel of the hands below the anklebone, one on the medial side and one on the lateral side, then move the hands rapidly back and forth. *The hands will be going in the opposite direction from each other.* The foot will shake from side to side. Be sure the hands are kept firmly against the foot so as not to burn the skin. (**See Figure 4.11**) After you become adept at this maneuver, you can try to slowly roll the heel of the hands from the lateral to the medial edge and then back as you rapidly move them back and forth.

ANKLE STRETCH "UNDER" (ACHILLES TENDON STRETCH)

Rest the right heel in the palm of the left hand. The thumb of the left hand will fit into the groove on the lateral part of the ankle where the leg is joined onto the foot (groin reflex). Next, place the heel of the right hand on the plantar surface of the foot on the 3rd, 4th and 5th metatarsal bones with the thumb and fingers lying horizontally and loosely across the metatarsals. Push the foot back as far as possible and then let it return in a slight oval motion via its natural spring to its neutral position. For optimal efficiency the right shoulder should be directly behind the working hand. Repeat 4 or 5 times in one direction and the same number of times in the other direction. Repeat this process on the left foot with the alternate hands. (**See Figures 4.12a, 4.12b**)

ANKLE STRETCH "OVER"

Coming from the lateral side of the foot, place the left hand with the fingers together over the dorsal side of the foot with the webbing between the thumb and fingers over the ankle joint where the foot is joined onto the leg. The rest of the fingers are wrapped around the leg. Place the heel of the right hand on the plantar surface of the foot on the 3th, 4th and 5th metatarsal bones with the thumb and fingers lying horizontally and loosely across the metatarsals. Push the foot back firmly with the heel of the hand and let it return, in a slight oval motion, via its own natural spring. For optimal efficiency the right shoulder should be directly behind the working hand.

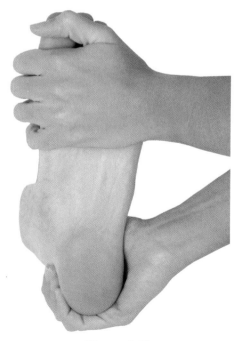

Figure 4.12a
Ankle stretch "under" relaxation technique

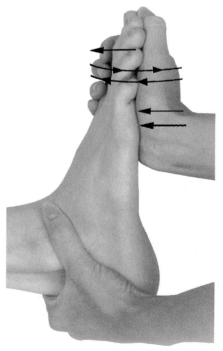

Figure 4.12b
Ankle stretch "under" relaxation technique

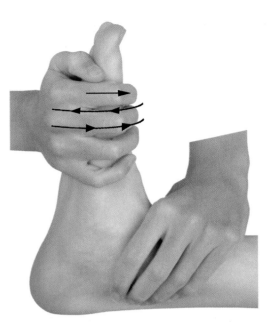

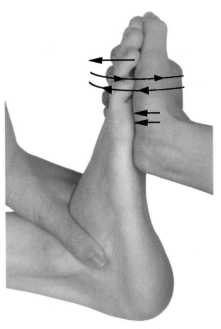

Figure 4.13a
Ankle stretch "over" relaxation technique

Figure 4.13b
Ankle stretch "over" relaxation technique

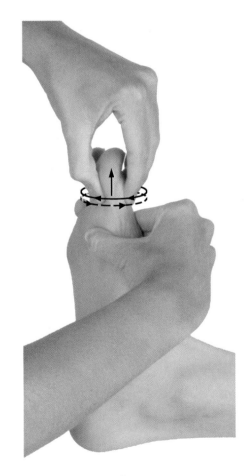

Figure 4.14
Toe rotation relaxation technique

Repeat in both directions several times. Repeat this process on the left foot with the alternate hands. (**See Figures 4.13a, 4.13b**)

TOE ROTATION

Hold the base of the toe you wish to rotate firmly with the thumb and fingers of the holding hand, the thumb on the plantar surface and the fingers on the dorsal surface. Take the thumb and 1st two fingers of your working hand and place them over the toe all the way to its base. With a slight lift, rotate each toe, first in one direction several times, and repeat in the opposite direction. (**See Figure 4.14**)

DIAPHRAGM–DEEP BREATHING

Place the ball of the thumbs in the center of the diaphragm/solar plexus reflex on both feet at the same time, allowing the fingers to comfortably support the dorsum of the foot. Ask your client to take a deep breath and maintain it each time you press on this reflex. Push in to this reflex as they take a deep breath and maintain the pressure while they hold their breath for a short time. As they slowly exhale, you should slowly let up on the pressure about halfway. Do this 4 or 5 times gradually increasing the time you hold the pressure and they hold their breath. Always maintain about half the pressure while they slowly exhale. It helps if you breathe with them. (**See Figure 4.15**) This technique is generally reserved for the end of a session.

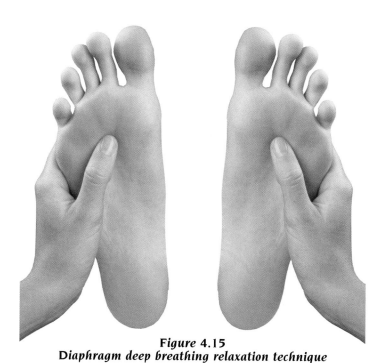

Figure 4.15
Diaphragm deep breathing relaxation technique

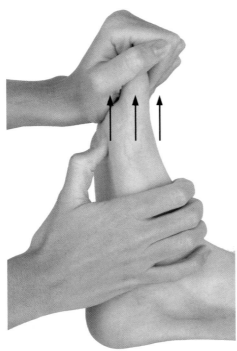 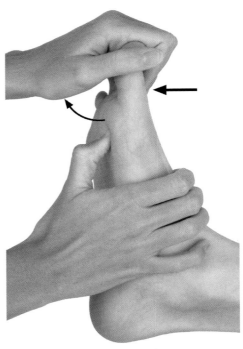

Figure 4.16a
Diaphragm tension relaxation technique

Figure 4.16b
Diaphragm tension relaxation technique

DIAPHRAGM/SOLAR PLEXUS TENSION RELAXER

In this relaxing technique, you will work the whole diaphragm reflex from medial to lateral with the foot slightly tipped out. Starting on the medial side of the foot, place the slightly bent working thumb on the base of the metatarsal head. Grasp the foot at the base of the toes with the holding hand, making sure the thumb and index finger are placed around the great toe. (**See Figure 4.16a**) It is important that the holding hand is placed squarely over the toes and not to the side. Lift the foot with the holding hand and then pull the metatarsals onto the thumb (applying extra pressure with the thumb). (**See Figure 4.16b**) The pressure of the pulling fingers should be on the dorsum of the foot at the base of the toes. When pulling the toes onto the thumb the heel of the holding hand should come slightly away from the plantar surface. Be careful not to bend the toes while doing this. The thumb should then take one small sideways step toward the lateral side and continue this process across the entire diaphragm/solar plexus reflex. Repeat the process several times. Continue until you reach the lateral edge.

INTRODUCTION TO THE SYSTEMS

The human body is composed of a myriad of parts working together for the good health of the entire being. These parts are usually grouped into systems: structures and organs related to each other to perform certain functions.

In the following chapters, each of these systems including their functions and integral parts are briefly discussed. This is followed by a detailed discussion concerning the reflex points of the components of these systems, their locations on the feet and the exact techniques used to work these reflexes.

In order to be a proficient Reflexologist one must understand each system of the body more fully. Do not restrict your study to just this volume. Anatomy and physiology of the human body require continual study as we are always learning new things.

These procedures will be described system by system. In our seminars we have found that this is the best method for learning. This, however, would not be the suggested order for giving a Reflexology session. For the proper sequence, **see Chapter 14**.

As most components of a system are found on both feet, I will simplify things by describing how to work on the system's reflex points on the **right foot throughout this book**. It should be noted that in working these reflexes I will start with the **right hand** as the working hand as I begin to work on the **right foot**. When the reflex for a specific organ is located only on the left foot, I will then work the left foot.

All of the reflexes associated with the systems are illustrated on the **foldout chart** located at the back of this book. The chart may be folded out for visibly studying it while reading the chapters.

Chapter 5

THE SKELETAL, NERVOUS, AND MUSCULAR SYSTEMS

"From whom the whole body fitly joined together and compacted by that which every joint supplieth . . .'

Ephesians 4:16

THE SKELETAL, NERVOUS, AND MUSCULAR SYSTEMS

As you practice Reflexology more and more, you will see that these three systems are so intimately related and interconnected that it would be beyond the scope of this book to divide and delve into each of the three. That task remains the challenge of the writers of anatomy books as well as those of the neurophysiologists.

However, I will touch upon some basic anatomy, nerve and muscle functions and suggest that you become familiar with some of the more prominent muscles as well as nerve plexus and bones. I would particularly recommend your becoming familiar with the bones of the foot since some of them are used for reference points throughout this book.

One thing I might add here is the thought that, as you study these three systems or, as a matter of fact, as you study all the systems of the body, it should become abundantly clear that the human body is truly a work of divine creation.

THE SKELETAL SYSTEM

Here is an assemblage of one of the busiest tissues in the body, a veritable chemical factory that is constantly busy and involved in processes which include the production of blood components, minerals and other vital materials. We don't usually think of our Skeletal System in that way. Most of us think of the bones as supporting the body and affording protection for the organs . . . 206 bones with the *neck bones connected to the shoulder bones*, and so on as the old song goes. Well, it is true that the Skeletal System **does** support and protect, but it also contributes a whole lot more to our well being. (**See Figure 5.1**) As a matter of fact, we seldom think of the bones as organs, but they are when you consider the medical definition of an organ as *"a somewhat independent part of the body that performs a special function or functions."*

Look at it this way: Bones act as a reservoir for most of the body's mineral needs including:

99% of the calcium

88% of the phosphorus, plus copper and cobalt.

And these structural *factories* work around the clock making the cellular elements of the blood.

When you consider that this body of yours uses up or depletes 180-million red blood cells in a single minute, and that the bones resupply most of their replacements, then you begin to see just how important those 206 bones are. In the bone marrow, red, white and platelet cells are manufactured every day. The bones also contain millions of cells called osteoblasts which produce a highly important form of protein called collagen, the matrix for new bone that is constantly being replenished by the body.

Then consider that all important mineral: calcium. It is released into the body from the bones when needed to supply vital functions. This is a very critical role which keeps a delicate balance in the body's chemical factory.

Last but not least, the bones serve as moorings for muscles. We would be unable to move if our muscles were not attached to bones via tendons and ligaments . . . those tough bands of connective tissue which hold those 206 bones and muscles together.

These connecting parts, the tendons and ligaments, are prone to injury, especially when they are used inappropriately and when one's nutrition is subpar. Thus, we experience strains and sprains. The Reflexologist must always consider the role that these tendons and ligaments play in injuries to the Skeletal System.

I should also mention *articulations*. The word is used to describe the connection of bone to bone within the Skeletal System and is usually divided into *movable* and *immovable* joints. The thing to remember here is that the movable joints contain a cavity filled with a joint lubricating fluid called *synovia*. The cavity containing the fluid is called a *bursa*. When the bursa of a joint in the great toe becomes inflamed, it thickens, the joint enlarges and sometimes *displaces* or makes the toe crooked . . . then a *bunion* is formed.

While on the subject of bones, it is important that the Reflexologist note the strik-

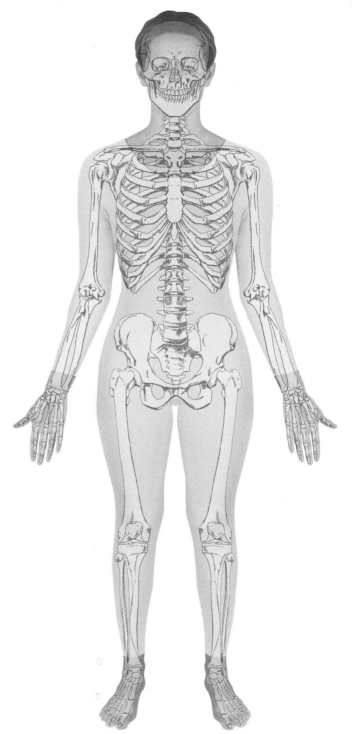

Figure 5.1
The skeletal system

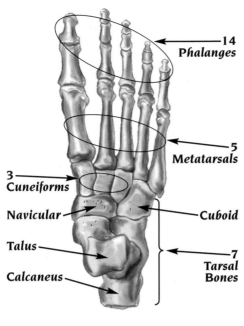

14
Phalanges

5
Metatarsals

3
Cuneiforms

Navicular

Cuboid

Talus

Calcaneus

7
Tarsal Bones

Figure 5.2
Bones of the foot

ing similarity and relationship of the shoulder to the hip, and the arm to the leg. We will be discussing these *referral areas* later when we talk about *working the reflexes* in this chapter.

THE FOOT

Almost one quarter of all the bones in the entire human body are located in the feet. (**See Figure 5.2**) Each foot is composed of 26 bones assembled into what has been called one of the most fantastic engineering accomplishments of all time. 26 bones, 107 ligaments and 19 muscles of each foot support and balance the rest of the body.

If we think of our feet as the foundation of our home, then we get a pretty good picture of just how important they are. If we don't have a solid foundation, the whole structure suffers. We know that when the feet are out of alignment, it can create a situation conducive to many health problems. For instance, if you walk favoring one foot over the other, you almost invariably throw your back out of alignment. Conversely, if the back or spine is out of alignment, you sometimes will walk favoring one side of the body and one foot, which leads to foot problems.

THE BONES OF THE FOOT

Some of the bones of the foot are of particular interest to the Reflexologist, including the tarsal bones which compare to the wrist bones. These are 7 in number and are in the heel and back part of the foot. The 5 long bones (the metatarsals) and the 14 bones (phalanges) of the toes correspond to the metacarpals of the hand and the phalanges of the fingers and thumbs, respectively. Get to know these bones of the foot, you will find that *familiarity breeds contentment*.

THE NERVOUS SYSTEM

No system in the human body exemplifies homeostasis better than the Nervous System . . . every cell of every nerve fiber must work in balance for maximum performance. The Nervous System is the intricate *link* to all systems of the human body. It can be compared to the wiring system in your house . . . when all the appliances work and the air conditioner or the heater is making life comfortable, we give little thought to that mass of wires, fuses and switches that are responsible for our feeling of well-being. But let something happen to that system and then we realize just how important these things are. The main components of this system are, of course, the brain and the spinal cord.

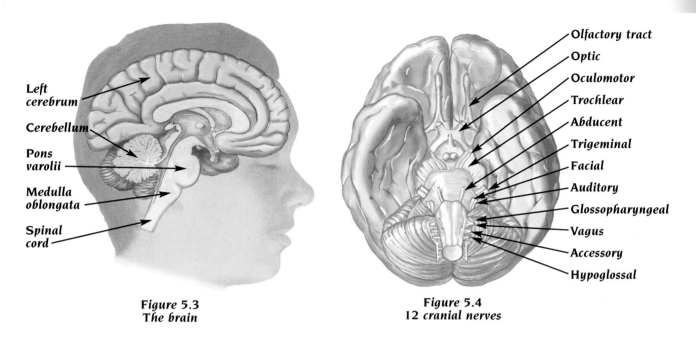

Figure 5.3
The brain

Figure 5.4
12 cranial nerves

THE BRAIN (See Figure 5.3)

It has been estimated that an electron tube computer would have to be the size of a New York City skyscraper to contain the equipment comparable to that in the 3 pounds or so of the human brain.

Every cell in the body is ruled by the brain . . . dreaming, speaking, thinking . . . even *changing our mind*.

Nearly 2500 years ago, Hippocrates, after studying head wounds, concluded that *the brain of man is double*, an astute observation, since the brain is composed of two symmetrical hemispheres. The left hemisphere of the brain controls the right side of the body while the right hemisphere controls the left side. This is the reason why, when someone is paralyzed on the right side, it is the left portion of the brain that has been damaged.

The medulla is called the *control center* of the brain as well as the *switchboard* since it is from this area that the 12 pairs of cranial nerves arise. These cranial nerves *connect* the body to the brain serving the sensory and motor needs of the head, neck, chest and abdomen. (**See Figure 5.4**)

Basically, the brain functions in many different ways:

- It **regulates** body activities as well as controlling them. It adjusts the body's mechanism for changes to internal or external conditions.

- It is the **center of consciousness**. It makes you aware of time and place, etc.

- It is the **seat of sensations**. It receives impulses from the sense organs: eyes, ears, nose, etc., and turns them into sensations of sight, hearing, smell, touch, etc.

- It is the **source of voluntary acts**.

- It is the **seat of our emotions**.

- It is the **center for thought, reasoning, memory** . . . all the so-called higher mental processes.

- And, it sits on another important **life line** . . . the spine.

THE SPINE–LIFELINE OF THE BODY

The spine is the center of the body and the center of more trouble and misery than almost any other structure you carry around in your being. That's probably because that articulated hollow group of odd-shaped bones is put under stress when you stand erect and have all that weight bearing down on it. And look what you make it do . . . bend, swivel, twist and contort to a point where it almost screams *enough*. Only when it has had more than enough does it let you know by the so-called *slipped disc*, lower back pain, etc.

Yet, this engineering marvel we call the spine has to be taken seriously if we realize that the hollow center carries a nerve system that would put any telephone company to shame. The spinal cord carries millions of messages back and forth from the brain and body . . . every conceivable motion you make is the result of an instantaneous message flashed through that direct line . . . 31 pairs of spinal nerves transmitting constantly. The spinal cord carries millions of messages back and forth from the brain and body. The spinal cord is protected against shock with a unique *shock absorber* called cerebrospinal fluid (CSF) and, of course, the bones or vertebrae which protect the whole system. But it doesn't even stop there . . . these vertebrae are able to twist and bend because they are *padded*. Each of these oddly-shaped bones rest on *pads called the intervertebral discs*, which are covered with a tough membranous envelope. (**See Figure 5.5**)

Acting as another natural *shock absorber* of the spine are the strange *curves* themselves. The spinal curves are designed in such a way that they actually absorb the daily shock that results from walking, running, or jogging . . . or even lifting that bag of groceries from the back of the car. Hundreds of muscles and almost a thousand ligaments are a constant working part of this system. Stress and tension can affect all of them or a series of them, enough to make *backache* a common household word.

Before we begin looking into the physiology and anatomy of the spine, it is interesting to note just how the spine relates to the structure of the feet.

The spine consists of 26 vertebrae; the feet have 26 bones. The adult spine has 4 curves; the sacral, lumbar, thoracic and the cervical. Each foot has 4 curves.

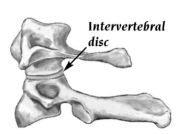

Figure 5.5
Intervertebral disc

Intervertebral disc

When I speak of the curves of the foot, I am referring to those curves along the medial longitudinal arch. If we place these curves against a lateral view of the spine, we can easily see how the curves of the spine match the curves of the feet. (**See Figure 5.6**)

The spine, or vertebral column, is a part of the axial

skeleton. It is a strong, flexible, rodlike structure which supports the head, gives attachments to the ribs, and encloses and protects the vital spinal cord.

The vertebrae are divided into 5 groups, according to their distinguishing characteristics. The cervical region has 7 vertebrae, the thoracic region has 12 vertebrae, the lumbar has 5 vertebrae, the sacral has 1 vertebra and the coccyx is made up of fused vertebrae. These vertebrae are all separated by intervertebral discs which are cushion-like structures that serve to absorb shock. They have a tough envelope of cartilage containing a jelly-like substance.

We hear so much these days about lower back pain. It is a universal plague. Many back pain sufferers attribute lower back pain to a "slipped disc". Most of the time, however, lower back pain has other origins such as weak muscles, asymmetrical posture, overweight, osteoporosis and many other conditions. Reflexology can help many lower back conditions including sciatica. The spine is supported by hundreds of muscles and ligaments. Lack of proper exercise, stress of life and poor posture are responsible for most of today's back problems.

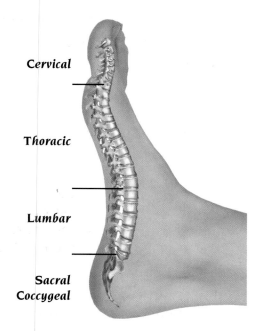

Cervical

Thoracic

Lumbar

Sacral
Coccygeal

Figure 5.6
Curves of the spine and foot

Without exercise, these muscles will weaken, and sitting over an office desk or slumping in an armchair watching television will produce uneven stress throughout the entire length of the spine.

"Structure Governs Function" is a common saying among osteopathic physicians. This is easy to understand when we realize that there are 31 pairs of spinal nerves originating from the spinal cord. They come out from the spinal cord and connect to the various organs, glands and structures throughout the entire body. The body's vital functions depend on an unimpeded nerve supply as well as an adequate blood supply if it is to perform at optimum level. When we study this awesome, complex network, we can readily understand the vital significance of *"Structures Governing Function."*

ABNORMAL TENSION OF MUSCLES OR LIGAMENTS on any vertebrae or group of vertebrae will cause pressure on a spinal nerve which supplies, for instance, the liver or kidneys. This pressure even though slight, may be enough over a period of time, sometimes even many years, to impair the nerve supply and circulation to those organs.

This spinal tension is caused by stress, **mental or physical**, and acts like a tourniquet upon the affected part whose function will be affected to a lesser or greater degree, but, in any instance, enough to affect homeostasis.

We can say here that since most back pain is associated with tension, we have in

Reflexology a very valuable modality in that one of its prime benefits is the reduction of tension or stress. Another point to remember is that we do not *just* work the spinal reflex areas for conditions associated with back pain, they should be worked often during all Reflexology sessions. This way, we are able to reduce any tension along the spine which would optimize the nerve and blood supply to other important parts of the body.

Always keep in mind that the spine is regarded as **one** organ. With that in mind, it is easy to see that whatever affects one end of it will also have an affect on the opposite end, and vice versa. Always work the entire spinal reflex.

Also, don't forget to include the helper areas for the spine which are the hip/sciatic, pelvic area, knee/leg, side of neck and the shoulder reflexes.

THE MUSCULAR SYSTEM

Many times I am asked why my discussion of the Muscular System is included with that of the Skeletal System. The reason is obvious since the two systems are so closely tied together in enabling the body to have locomotion and body posture as well as manipulation of the fingers, the eyes, the tongue, etc.

For our purposes here, we will define the Muscular System as that part of the body that contracts and relaxes giving the body movement and posture. Besides the muscles themselves, we are going to include the tendons and ligaments.

Muscle functions are usually divided into two kinds: voluntary and involuntary.

While sometimes this division of muscle function is hazy, let's accept the definition and look at the functions this way.

The voluntary functions include the maintenance of proper posture and those movements which are readily visible, including the limbs and fingers. The toes play an important part in balance and locomotion. The diaphragm which is a large umbrella-shaped muscular band is necessary for respiration; as the pharynx is needed for swallowing. The tongue and lips enable us to eat and speak; the abdominal wall assists in breathing and elimination. All of these muscular structures are under voluntary control.

Involuntary muscular functions include the movement of food through the digestive tract called peristalsis. It also includes the movement of bile from the gallbladder, urine from the kidneys and the contractions of the uterus. Other involuntary functions include the regulation of the size of openings in the pupil of the eye or the neck of the bladder. And then there is the opening of blood vessels and the bronchioles in the lungs . . . all of them regulated without our even trying.

A few words about *fatigue*.

All of us have experienced this tired sensation which is often felt in the muscles. It is usually defined as the inability of the muscle to perform work. There are several factors which are responsible for this type of sensation:

- Excessive activity: this is a definite cause of fatigue and rest will cure it.

- Inadequate activity: this often goes unrecognized, it underlies the fact that most people feel better when they exercise.

- Malnutrition: caused by lack of proper foods, especially proteins, minerals and vitamins.

- Circulatory disturbances: when insufficient oxygen, glucose and nutrients get to the muscles and when the blood cannot remove waste products, fatigue occurs in the affected muscles.

- Respiratory disturbance: when the oxygen/carbon dioxide ratio is upset as in emphysema.

- Infections: cause fatigue since the energies of the body are used to fight the infection.

- Endocrine gland disturbances: as seen in menopause, diabetes, thyroid and adrenal disorders.

- Other factors include poor posture and some cases of eyestrain.

THE EFFECT OF EXERCISE ON THE MUSCULAR SYSTEM

Activity as found in a sound program of exercise brings about a profound effect on the muscles of the body; but even more importantly, nearly every other system of the body is affected also. Heart rate, respiration, perspiration and the skeletal framework all respond to exercise. The ability of the muscles to take up and utilize oxygen depends on their use. As I always say *"What we don't use . . . we lose"*. So a planned program of regular exercise is a must for full performance of bodily systems.

WORKING THE REFLEXES FOR THE SKELETAL, NERVOUS, AND MUSCULAR SYSTEMS

In selecting a working sequence for this section, it was only natural that I should follow the subject of our discussion . . . the anatomy of the body. So, we will begin with the highest structure, of course, the brain and then work through the spine and the muscles to the feet.

WORKING THE BRAIN

The main focal areas for working the brain are the tips of the great toes, since each represents one-half of the head. This, of course, does not exclude the tips of the small toes since they aid in *fine-tuning* anything in the head.

Hold the right great toe with the thumb and index finger of the right hand. The 1st joint of the index finger of the left hand will be resting on the tip of the thumb. This stabilizes the index finger which is used to work across the tip of the great toe in a rolling motion with the wrist. (**See Figure 5.7**) Start with the lateral edge of the tip of the index finger and roll across the tip of the great toe. Pick up the index finger and move to where you finished and repeat this process until the entire tip of the great toe is covered. Repeat this entire process several times on both feet. This technique maybe applied with either hand.

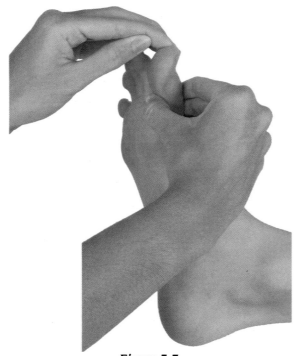

Figure 5.7
Working the brain reflex

SECTIONS OF THE SPINE

The guidelines are of great importance in order for us to accurately locate certain vertebrae. This is quite understandable since we are all unique in our physical makeup.

The reflex areas for the spine are located on the medial edge of both feet . . . the right foot corresponding to the right side of the spine; the left foot to the left side of the spine. (**See Figure 5.8**)

I recommend working up and down the spinal reflex area each time, thus covering a slightly different portion of the spine; the reason becomes evident when we realize that the spinal reflex is a relatively wide structure. Also, you must be sure that you work **across** each of these areas because sometimes a reflex may be sensitive in one direction and not in another. Therefore working the spinal reflex in many different directions is very important considering all the nerves that serve the body have their origin from the spine.

SACRUM–COCCYX REFLEX

One of the most difficult reflexes to work is the sacral/coccyx reflex which is located in the section of the foot from the back of the heel to the pelvic guideline on the medial edge.

It is here, at the sacrum and coccyx as well as the lower lumbar vertebrae, on the lower end of the spine where many injuries are manifested. It is an *inherent weakness* in many people and *lower back pain* is a constant source of distress. As a matter of fact, there are very few of us who haven't injured our back

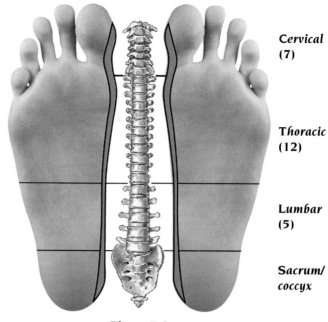

Cervical (7)

Thoracic (12)

Lumbar (5)

Sacrum/ coccyx

Figure 5.8
The spinal reflex compared to the spinal vertebrae

at one time or another. When we do injure a certain area, there is a buildup of inflammation that occurs from the trauma so you will usually find that the lower back reflex area will be sensitive on most people. While this does not necessarily indicate serious problems in all cases, it may reflect congestion, possibly from previous injuries. As I so often have stated in my seminars: remember, if one end of the spine is affected, it often affects the opposite end. As we work the lower portion of the spinal reflex, it will often help the neck region and many headaches that are caused by lower back problems.

The spine remains a vital area to the Reflexologist, and especially the lower back for such conditions as migraine headache, constipation, prostate and female disorders. Many times these are manifestations of stress or tension which have "settled" in the spine.

After all, the spine is the center of the body's equilibrium as it holds us erect, and is surrounded by muscles, ligaments, tendons and nerves. When tension builds up and perhaps pulls a set of muscles, the entire body reacts to fight that tension. Some people describe it as *"their back being out"* . . . it is simply muscles pulling on the spine as a result of tension. Certainly, subluxations may occur meaning the vertebrae are out of proper alignment. Remember, bones don't move by themselves – only when pulled by muscles, muscles that are tense, more tense than they should be.

When working this portion of the foot, you will usually find that the skin is tough and callused. This is one of those special areas where **leverage** is so important. Using the fingers of the working hand around the lateral side of the heel for leverage is so important since it gives the hand firmness and authority as well as facilitating a smooth, even pressure on this reflex.

When working the sacrum/coccyx area, you must realize you are working the base of the spine. Apart from working for lower back pain, you also contact the nerve supply to the pelvic area for conditions such as hemorrhoids, anal itch and sacroiliac strain, in fact, any structure that has its nerve innervation from this part of the spine may be affected.

LUMBAR REFLEX

The 5th lumbar reflex is located at the pelvic guideline. (**See Figure 5.8**) From this point up to the waistline guideline is the lumbar reflex, which is of great importance in working conditions such as lower back pain, constipation, bladder problems, prostate disorders, female problems and for consequent benefit to all the structures in the abdominal area due to their nerve innervations.

Most injuries to the lower spine will involve the 4th and 5th lumbar vertebrae because they support more of the body weight than any other vertebrae. Sciatic pain is also helped by working the lumbar and sacral reflexes thoroughly, as the sciatic nerve originates from the 4th and 5th lumbar vertebrae as well as the sacrum, and it is the largest nerve in the body.

THORACIC REFLEX

The thoracic reflex is located from the waistline guideline up to the point where the great toe joins the foot and is made up of 12 vertebrae. (**See Figure 5.8**) Mental stress can affect this area greatly, as well as poor posture. As in any other section or part of the spine, tension can impede the nerve supply to all the corresponding organs. A few of the organs involved in this area are: the lungs, heart, liver, spleen and the kidneys.

The heart, for instance, is supplied by many nerves that originate in the thoracic section of the spine. We can see how important it is to work the spinal reflex thoroughly in **every session** to help promote an unimpeded nerve function and not just in the treatment of back pain.

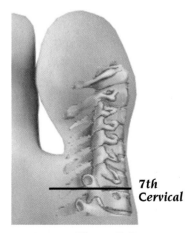

7th
Cervical

Figure 5.9
7th cervical reflex

CERVICAL REFLEX

The cervical reflex is located from the base of the great toe, where the toe joins the foot, up to the top medial edge opposite the root of the toenail. (**See Figure 5.8**) There are 7 cervical vertebrae, the top one supports the skull and is called the Atlas and is the 1st cervical vertebra; the 2nd cervical vertebra is the Axis. The 12 cranial nerves come off just above the cervicals. The major ones will be the optic, olfactory, vagus, auditory and facial nerves. The lowest cervical vertebra is the 7th cervical which protrudes at the back of the neck and can usually be easily felt. (**See Figure 5.9**)

Working the cervical reflex is always important in the adjunctive treatment of such conditions as ear, eye, nose and facial problems such as Bell's Palsy and Epilepsy. The 6th and 7th cervical vertebrae reflexes are important to work in all arm, hand, neck and shoulder problems, including whiplash injury and carpal tunnel syndrome.

WORKING THE SPINAL REFLEX

You will find that *tipping* the foot out is very important when working the spinal reflex. Use the right hand on the right foot (working hand) and the holding hand will be in the basic holding position.

Start by working the sacral/coccyx area. Roll the thumb over the edge of the heel (often a callused area) and walk up approximately one half inch towards the leg. (**See Figure 5.10**) The entire sacral-coccyx area is covered using this technique. Then start by using the right thumb and begin to *walk* up the sacral/coccyx reflex from the base of the heel to approximately the pelvic guideline or as far as the hand can reach. (**See Figure 5.11**) Note how the fingers of the working hand are placed on the lateral side of the heel, opposite the thumb in order to obtain the needed leverage. Repeat several times on a slightly different path, covering all sides of the reflex and never losing contact with the foot.

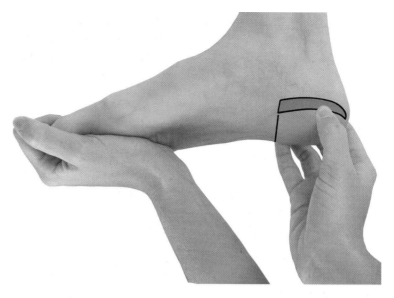

Figure 5.10
Working across the sacral-coccyx reflex

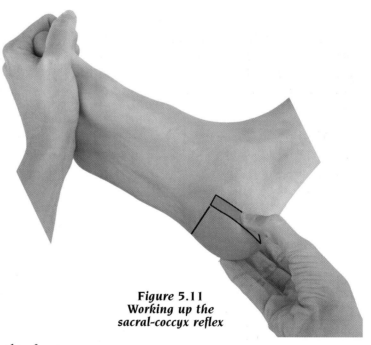

Figure 5.11
Working up the
sacral-coccyx reflex

Work the lumbar reflex by placing the fingers over the top of the foot and the thumb remains approximately on the pelvic guideline. (**See Figure 5.12**) Walk up the lumbar reflex to the waistline guideline and then continue walking the thoracic reflex until reaching the 7th cervical reflex, located below the base of the great toe. (**See Figure 5.13**) It is important to move the leverage fingers so that they stay more or less opposite the thumb, otherwise the strength in the thumb diminishes. Repeat

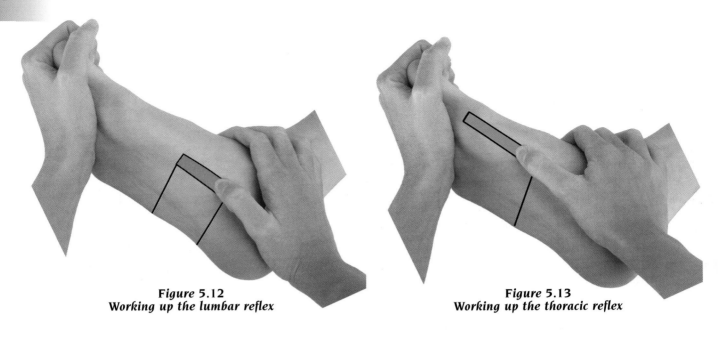

Figure 5.12
Working up the lumbar reflex

Figure 5.13
Working up the thoracic reflex

several times changing position slightly to cover the entire area.

It is best to use the index finger when working the cervical reflex for an extra fine treatment. Start by supporting the foot with the fingers of the left hand which are placed over the toes and hold the great toe **firmly** with the thumb and index finger. The working hand then supports the foot with the thumb and the 3rd, 4th and 5th fingers while the index finger walks from the base of the great toe to the base of the nail. (**See Figure 5.14**) Repeat this several times then change direction in order to work across the same reflex. (**See Figure 5.15**) The leverage of the working hand will have

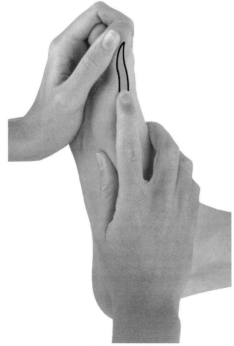

Figure 5.14
Working up the cervical reflex

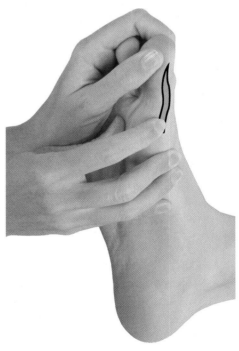

Figure 5.15
Working across the cervical reflex

to be adjusted in order to achieve this. It is important to note that without sufficient support the index finger will be ineffective.

Work down the spinal reflex by supporting the foot on the metatarsal pad with the fingers pointing upwards and bent at the knuckle joints. Use the thumb of the working hand to walk all the way down the spinal reflex. (**See Figure 5.16**) Repeat several times using a slightly different path each time. This procedure will be repeated on the left foot.

HIP/SCIATIC REFLEX

Place the heel of the right foot on the 3rd and 4th fingers of the left hand with the index finger resting underneath the lateral side of the anklebone and the thumb on the bottom of the heel for leverage. Place the holding hand on the metatarsal padding, keeping the foot back and straight. (**See Figure 5.17**) Walk with the index finger in a forward motion angling at an approximate 45° angle into the anklebone. Go approximately one quarter to one half inch, stop, lift up, come back and start over. Repeat this process several times. Change hands, then place the right heel on the palm of the right hand with the 3rd finger resting under the anklebone on the lateral side of the foot. Walk it toward you, about one quarter to one half inch. (**See Figure 5.18**) This time the left holding hand will be placed on the metatarsal pad holding the foot back and straight.

Repeat this procedure working the opposite foot with the alternate hand. It must be noted that this is a **touch** reflex and is very sensitive. You **must** keep the foot back and straight to work it adequately. If you tip the foot towards the medial side to see what you are doing (as most people will be tempted to do) it will tighten up the tendons and will not allow you to reach the reflex area which is sensitive on most people.

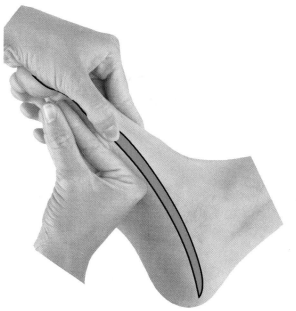

Figure 5.16
Working down the spinal reflex

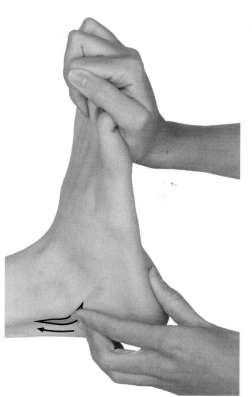

Figure 5.17
Working up the sciatic reflex

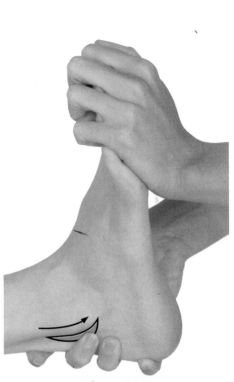

Figure 5.18
Working down the sciatic reflex

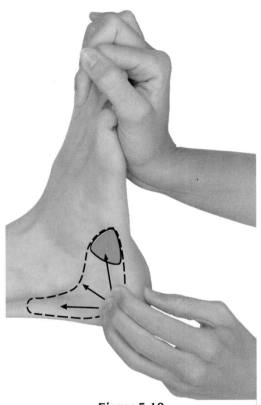

Figure 5.19
Working the pelvic reflex area

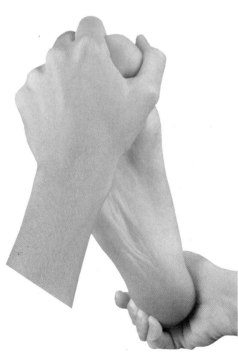

Figure 5.20a
*Working the pelvic area using
the pivot rolling technique*

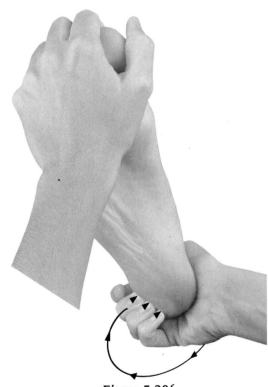

Figure 5.20b
*Working the pelvic area using
the pivot rolling technique*

PELVIC REFLEX AREA

Work the pelvic area by keeping the foot back and straight, using the basic holding technique. Place the thumb of the working hand on the heel for leverage. Using all fingers, work the entire pelvic area in many directions by changing the angle of the wrist. (**See Figure 5.19**)

Another useful method for extra contact is the Pivot Rolling Technique, use the 3rd, 4th and 5th fingers instead of the thumb to walk up from the base of the heel. Place the thumb muscle of the working hand on the medial side of the heel, which will be used as the point of '*pivot*'. (**See Figure 5.20a**) Now pivot the hand simultaneously as you walk the 3rd, 4th and 5th fingers on the lateral side of the heel. Walk the fingers with each pivot. (**See Figure 5.20b**) This technique enables you to achieve considerable pressure with minimum effort. You can only walk up a short way with this method, but it is very effective for achieving extra strength to this tough area.

This is a helper area for the lower back as it works on all the muscles of the pelvic region, plus it encompasses the hip and sciatic reflexes. (**See Figure 5.21**) The sciatic nerve is the main nerve which comes through the hip area and down the leg. Remember that this is also a referral area for shoulder problems.

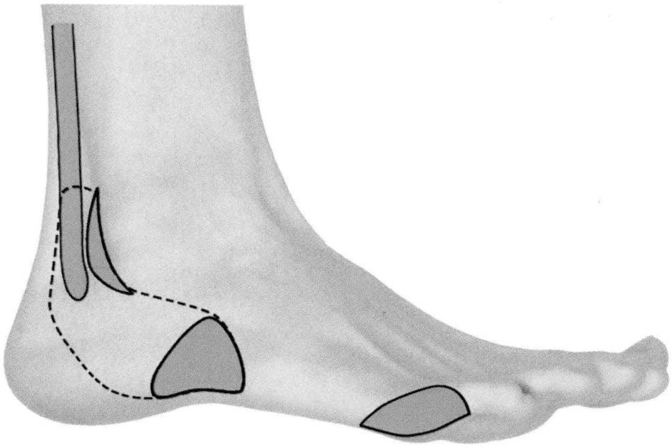

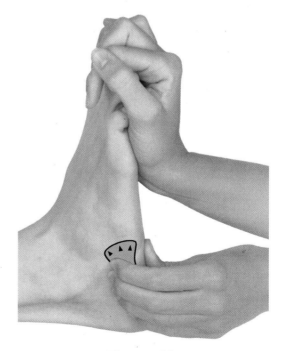

Figure 5.21
Helper areas for the spine

KNEE/LEG REFLEX

The other helper area for the lower back is the knee/leg reflex area which is located from the base of the 5th metatarsal on the little toe side to the beginning of the heel on the lateral edge of the foot (pelvic guideline). (**See Figure 5.21**) To work this reflex, the fingers can be used very effectively and thus save the thumb from overuse. Use the basic holding technique. Place the fingers of the left hand on the lateral edge of the dorsal surface and the thumb on the heel area for leverage. Walk the fingers in several directions by changing the angle of the wrist. (**See Figure 5.22**) Use the index finger, middle finger or **both** fingers simultaneously to work this area. Also use the alternate hand and come over the top of the foot working toward the lateral edge with the fingers.

Figure 5.22
Working the knee reflex

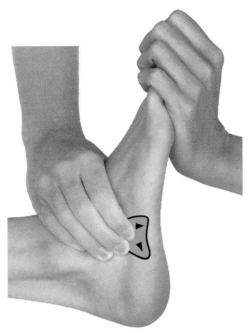

Figure 5.23
Working down the knee reflex

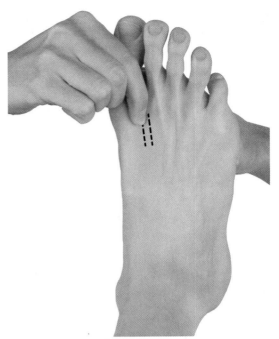

Figure 5.24
Working for whiplash (dorsal surface)

(**See Figure 5.23**) This reflex is found on both feet, an excellent area for knee and leg problems. This area is often *tender* and will usually be extremely sensitive on persons with these problems.

Keep these helper areas in mind since they are extremely useful when the lower back is involved.

COMMON AILMENTS

Some common ailments you should become familiar with:

BURSITIS

Inflammation of the bursa. Examples: Tennis elbow, housemaid's knee, bursitis of the shoulder.

When these conditions prevail, spend a little extra time on the reflex to the afflicted area. A helper area would be the adrenal glands.

ARTHRITIS

Enlargement of the bones around the joints.

There are so many causes for arthritis that I will not attempt to limit the areas to be worked. All the reflexes are involved. As with bursitis, a little extra attention should be given to the reflexes to the afflicted areas as well as all the glands.

WHIPLASH

An important area, especially for whiplash, is the area between the 1st and 2nd toe on the dorsal side of the foot. This is the best area to work for whiplash. Start with the right hand on the right foot. The holding hand will push firmly on the metatarsal pad, helping to spread the toes. The index finger of the right hand will walk down at a slight angle in this groove. Keep the fingers together for leverage. (**See Figure 5.24**) Walk down several times, making several passes between the great toe and the 2nd toe. Lift, do not drag the finger back. If you bend your finger excessively, you will dig in with your fingernails. Now, repeat this procedure with the left hand. The same technique is used on the left foot.

SHOULDER REFLEX

Neck conditions will often affect the shoulder, and the shoulder may affect the neck. Example: If you were to fall on your shoulder, there is a possibility of causing trauma to your neck.

When working the right shoulder reflex, use the left thumb around the little toe joint.

Keep the foot straight; the right holding hand will be supporting the toes and the thumb will be pushing the small toe back and slightly spreading it. This is important as this opens the 4th and 5th metatarsal bones. The left thumb will start at the diaphragm guideline and work across the 5th metatarsal bone, repeat until you have reached the base of the small toe. Give a little extra pressure once you have reached the area between the 5th and 4th toes. (**See Figure 5.25**) If the toes are not pushed back, the little toe will come forward and not allow you to get into the joint between the 4th and 5th toes. Repeat this several times. Change hands and repeat the process on the left foot.

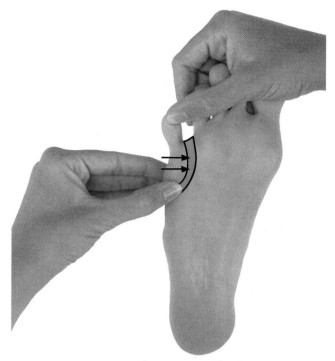

Figure 5.25
Working across the shoulder reflex

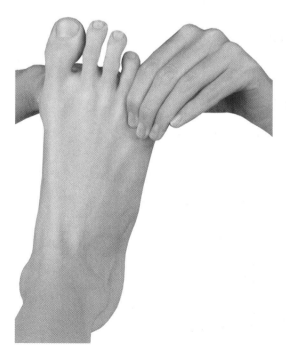

Figure 5.26
Working the shoulder reflex (dorsal surface)

59

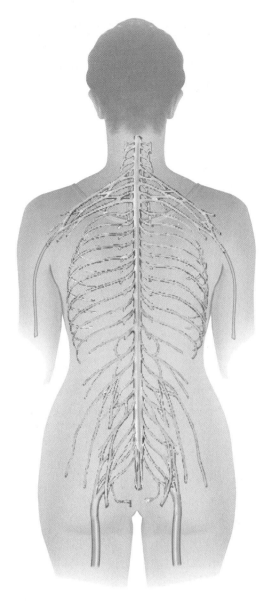

Figure 5.27
Spinal nerves

The shoulder reflex can also be worked straight up towards the toes from the diaphragm guideline to the base of the 5th toe on the plantar surface of the foot.

Work the top or dorsal part of the foot with the index finger on the opposite side from where the thumb worked. (**See Figure 5.26**) The finger will be placed on the top of the foot between the 4th and 5th toes and the thumb will push on the bottom of the foot toward the walking finger. The finger will walk down, starting at the base of the 4th and 5th toes, stop, lift up and work down again. Keep the fingers together resting them on the foot for support and leverage. Maintain pressure on the bottom of the foot, otherwise the foot will *cave in* and you won't have enough finger pressure. Also work the lateral edge of the little toe joint with the thumb. This area can also be worked for the arm. Repeat the process on the left foot with the alternate hand. The shoulder reflex is also a referral area for the hip.

AREAS OF THE SPINE AND THEIR RELATED NERVE INNERVATION

There are 31 pairs of nerves which pass through the vertebrae of the spine. These spinal nerves receive sensations from the sense organs and they carry motor instructions to the muscles and glands of the body. Becoming familiar with the spinal nerves, their distribution, and related clinical conditions can be of great help to the Reflexologist. (**See Figure 5.27**)

THE CERVICAL AREA

Eight (8) pairs of nerves move through this area and are very influential in affecting areas of the face and head. (The 1st and 2nd are coming from the 1st cervical vertebra). The following list describes the cervical nerves, followed by the vertebra they are coming from. Example: C-1 is the 1st cervical vertebra, C-2 is the 2nd cervical vertebra.

NERVE	INNERVATION	RELATED CONDITIONS
1st and 2nd Cervical C-1	Head, pituitary gland, scalp, brain, face, ear, sympathetic nervous system	Head colds, headaches, fainting, chronic tiredness, dizziness, muscle tension, high blood pressure, insomnia, migraine
3rd Cervical C-2	Eyes, sinuses, tongue, forehead, mastoids	Sinus trouble, allergies, ear trouble, eye trouble
4th Cervical C-3	Cheeks, teeth, ears	Neuritis, eczema, acne, ear troubles
5th Cervical C-4	Nose, lips, mouth, eustachian tube	Hay fever, catarrh, blocked eustachian tubes
6th Cervical C-5	Neck glands, pharynx, heart, vocal cords	Hoarseness, sore throat, etc.
7th Cervical C-6	Neck, shoulder muscles, tonsils, heart	Stiff neck, pain in the arm, croup, tonsillitis
8th Cervical C-7	Thyroid, shoulders and elbow, heart	Bursitis, thyroid problems

THE THORACIC AREA

Twelve (12) pairs of nerves pass through this area of the spine and all influence a great number of organs and glands in the upper trunk area, they also have an effect on the hands and arms.

NERVE	INNERVATION	RELATED CONDITIONS
1st Thoracic T-1	Lower arms from the elbow, wrists, hands, fingers, esophagus, wind pipe, heart	Asthma, coughs, breathing difficulties, pain below the elbows and in the hand
2nd Thoracic T-2	Heart, coronary arteries	Chest pain, functional heart conditions
3rd Thoracic T-3	Lungs, bronchial tubes (respiration area), pleura, chest, heart, breast	Pleurisy, pneumonia, the grippe, bronchitis
4th Thoracic T-4	Gallbladder, common bile duct, heart	Jaundice, gallbladder problems, shingles
5th Thoracic T-5	Solar plexus, liver, heart	Fever, low blood pressure, anemia, arthritis, adverse liver conditions
6th Thoracic T-6	Stomach	Indigestion, heart burn, nervous stomach
7th Thoracic T-7	Pancreas, duodenum	Ulcers, diabetes, often gastritis
8th Thoracic T-8	Spleen, diaphragm	Leukemia, hiccoughs

NERVE	INNERVATION	RELATED CONDITIONS
9th Thoracic T-9	Adrenal glands	Allergies, hives, an inadequate reaction to stress
10th Thoracic T-10	Kidneys	Kidney trouble, fatigue, hardening of the arteries
11th Thoracic T-11	Kidneys, ureters	Skin disorders, auto intoxication (absorption of poison from the gastrointestinal canal)
12th Thoracic T-12	Small intestines, fallopian tubes, lymph circulation	Gas pains, rheumatism, lymphatic congestion

THE LUMBAR, SACRAL AND COCCYX AREAS

This area of the spine has nerves supplying the lower area of the body and the legs.

NERVE	INNERVATION	RELATED CONDITIONS
1st Lumber L-1	Colon, groin area	Inflammation of the colon, constipation, hernia, diarrhea
2nd Lumbar L-2	Abdomen and its contents, appendix, blind pouch (cecum), the thighs	Cramps, appendicitis, varicose veins, breathing difficulties
3rd Lumbar L-3	Reproductive glands, urinary bladder, knee	Bladder trouble, painful or irregular menstrual periods, change of life symptoms, knee pains, involuntary discharge of urine, impotency
4th Lumbar L-4	Muscles of the lower back, sciatic nerve, prostate gland	Lumbago, backaches, too frequent urination, sciatica
		NOTE: The sciatic is the largest nerve in the body and affects nearly the whole of the leg, muscles of the back of the thigh and the foot
5th Lumbar L-5	Lower legs, ankles, feet, toes, arches	Cold feet, weakness and poor circulation in the legs, weak or swollen ankles, leg cramps
The Sacrum	Hip bone, buttocks	Curvature of the spine, sacroiliac strain
The Coccyx	Rectum, anus	Hemorrhoids, pain at the end of spine, anal itch

NOTE: In reviewing the spinal chart, it is well to note that very few of the conditions listed here are wholly under the control of any one nerve.

IN SUMMARY

The entire body below the neck, including the arms and the legs, is controlled by the spinal cord. Sensations from body parts traverse the spinal nerves, enter the spinal cord and then are relayed to the brain and other spinal centers. Messages from the cord or from the brain exit via spinal nerves to control the action of blood vessels, muscles and glands. From a simple reflex arc to the most deliberately planned activity, the spinal cord and its nerves serve the body every minute of every day.

Whenever there is impingement or entrapment of spinal nerves, serious body dysfunctions may occur. Pressure on the nerves may be due to injuries, tight (hypertonic) muscles, fibrotic scar tissue, vertebral subluxations and other causes.

Reflexology can nudge the body toward better functioning by improving lymphatic drainage, circulation and muscle relaxation. The wise Reflexologist will never forget the spine and its integral effects upon the whole body.

A WORD ON MUSCULAR TENSION

Tension is manifested many times in the trapezius and deltoid muscles of the back and shoulders. I have developed a particularly effective Reflexology technique for this specific area through years of practice and work on this widespread affliction.

For tension in the neck muscles, work the lateral side of the great toe. For all of the affected areas, including the trapezius and deltoids, work across the top of the foot from the great toe to the little toe in the metatarsal areas, particularly the grooves between the toes.

I generally find it is more effective to work the dorsal area of the foot although you **can** work the plantar area, but, since it is made up of a tougher layer of skin, the dorsal area seems more effective. However, I would recommend that you work both **the dorsal and plantar areas**.

Tension is also relieved by working the diaphragm/solar plexus reflex area. Work across this area with the standard thumb technique. Another technique I have developed for this area is the Diaphragm/Solar Plexus Tension Relaxer. Put the thumb on this area, then lift and pull the foot **onto** the thumb, move the thumb a bit, stop, lift and pull the foot onto the thumb, etc. Work in this manner across the entire reflex area. (**See Figure 5.28**) **See Chapter 4**, Relaxing Techniques, for a full description.

For numbness in the arms and hands I find that, besides working the neck and cervical

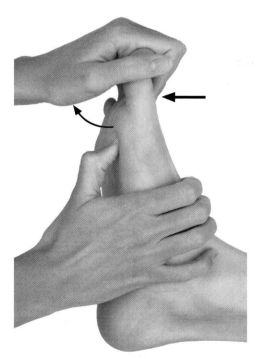

Figure 5.28
Diaphragm tension relaxation technique

reflexes, working the shoulder reflex often helps.

For lower back and leg complaints, always work the sciatic nerve reflex. A referral area for leg muscles would be to work the corresponding area on the arm.

A NOTE TO REMEMBER: Whenever you work the muscles, always remember that it is the adrenal glands that give the body's muscles their tone . . . always be sure to work the adrenal glands.

COMMON FOOT DISORDERS

CORNS AND CALLUSES

If a person's spine or hip is out of alignment, this situation can cause corns and calluses. Through many years of experience, I can usually tell a person's health and general condition by looking at their feet. This is especially true where there are conditions of deformity or extra growth of corns and/or calluses.

These conditions could quite easily be affecting the reflexes in that area, which in turn could affect the organs, glands or parts of the body associated with it.

When a Reflexologist notes such conditions as corns or calluses, extra work is needed to help these areas. However, if there is a preponderance of such conditions, it is usually suggested that they be treated by a podiatrist. It has been my experience that, once the corns and calluses have been removed by a podiatrist, working this region helps to alleviate the condition and they do not return as easily as before.

Many times they do not reappear **at all**.

A note on the particular condition of corns. It is more difficult working with corns because the area is frequently very sensitive. My recommended method is to work around the area to ease the pain of this condition first, then as you work, it becomes less sensitive and you will find that you can work the entire area.

BUNIONS

Inflammation and thickening of the bursa of the joint of the great toe are called bunions. To work for a bunion, hold the great toe with the holding hand, lightly pulling the great toe to straighten it. With the working thumb, use the basic thumb technique and work all around and then directly on the bunion. This area could be worked on every day. A little self help would be beneficial.

SPURS

While discussing bones of the feet, it might be well to touch upon one particular problem area . . . the calcaneal spur. (**See Figure 5.29**) These are formed by a mineral buildup on the end of the calcaneus bone in the heel. The Reflexologist must work

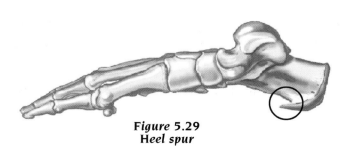
Figure 5.29
Heel spur

this area with a special zeal.

It should be noted that this particular procedure causes some discomfort but is very effective. With spurs, you should schedule regular sessions every day, or at least every other day. Begin by lightly working the area **around** the spur with the regular thumb technique. Gradually working up to and on the spur itself, you should gradually increase the pressure during the session. Once the area is loosened up you can then use the hook-in, back-up technique directly on the spur.

If you approach the area properly and come in on the area from every direction by using alternate thumbs over the spot and also use a lot of ankle rotating motions, you will help to improve the circulation to that area. This, in turn, helps nature to remove the microscopic waste products and carry them through the bloodstream.

Remember: For best results, this region could be worked every day. This is one of those rare exceptions where it is not necessary to give a full treatment each time you work on this condition.

FOR BROKEN BONES

To review our discussion in **Chapter 2,** where I compare the arm to the leg, etc., it is obvious that you will not work directly on a broken foot, instead, work the corresponding area of the hand with the basic thumb and finger technique. All referral areas are worked on the same side as the injury and you would follow a distinct regimen including:

- for a broken hand, work the corresponding area of the foot.

- for a broken leg, work the corresponding area of the arm at the corresponding site of the break.

- for a broken arm, work the corresponding area of the leg.

- for a broken finger, work the corresponding area of the toe.

Once this becomes clear, you should be able to immediately grasp the significance of referral areas. Always remember that it is easier to work the arm for leg problems than it is to work the leg for arm problems. This is primarily due to the heavy muscular structure of the leg making it difficult to reach the reflexes.

In the case of a sprain, a trained Reflexologist will immediately work the referral area in order to help stop inflammation and swelling. After the area shows signs of improvement, a light and direct application will serve to improve circulation and thus aid in the healing process.

This chapter is an extremely important one and one which should be read and reread since the spine, nerves and muscles play such an important part in Reflexology.

Now, let's take a specific look at some particular disorders and corresponding reflex areas to work.

DISORDERS OF THE SKELETAL SYSTEM

DISORDER	DESCRIPTION	REFLEX AREAS TO WORK
Ankylosis	Abnormal immobility and fixation of a joint.	Directly on the area, referral area (arm or leg), area on the foot
Arthritis	Ailments involving joints, muscles and tendons; also called "rheumatism".	Reflex to the region most affected, kidneys, all glands, diaphragm, work entire foot
Bunion	Inflammation and thickening of the bursa of the joint of the great toe.	Work around and directly on the bunion
Bursitis	Inflammation of a bursa: in the patella joint, it is called "housemaid's knee"; the elbow, "tennis elbow"; the shoulder, "bursitis".	Reflex to affected area, adrenals, parathyroids, the referral area to affected area
Fracture	A crack or break in an arm, leg or any bone.	Reflex to affected area on the foot, referral area in either the arm or leg, parathyroids, diaphragm
Gout	Acute arthritis and inflammation of a joint.	Reflex to affected area, kidneys, all glands
Scoliosis	Lateral curvature of the spine.	Reflex to the whole spine, all glands, chest/lung, shoulder

DISORDERS OF THE NERVOUS SYSTEM

DISORDER	DESCRIPTION	REFLEX AREAS TO WORK
Bell's Palsy	Paralysis of a facial nerve.	All toes, cervicals, neck, diaphragm, parathyroids
Encephalitis	Inflammation of the brain and its covering.	All toes, all glands: esp. adrenal
Epilepsy	A disorder of the nervous system; major symptom is convulsive seizures.	All toes, cervicals, neck, all glands, diaphragm

DISORDER	DESCRIPTION	REFLEX AREAS TO WORK
Headache	One of the most common ailments of man and is a symptom rather than a disorder; most result from vasodilation of blood vessels in tissues surrounding the brain or from tension in neck or scalp muscles; stress on whole body.	All toes, whole spine: esp. cervicals and lower spine, diaphragm, all glands
Hiccoughs	Spasmodic involuntary contractions of the diaphragm that result in uncontrolled breathing in of air.	Diaphragm, esophagus, stomach
Insomnia	Sleeplessness: an inability to fall asleep easily or to remain asleep.	Diaphragm, all glands: esp. pineal
Meningitis	Inflammation of the meninges that cover the brain and spinal cord.	All toes, whole spine, all glands
Morton's Neuroma	Also called plantar neuroma, Morton's disease or neuralgia which is caused by chronic compression of the nerve between the metatarsal heads.	Stretch the metatarsal heads, work around and then directly on the neuroma on both the plantar and dorsal side
Multiple Sclerosis	A disease causing hardened patches through-out the brain and spinal cord interfering with nerves in those areas.	Whole spine, all glands, all toes, diaphragm
Parkinson's disease	Disease of the brain causing stiffness of the muscles and characterized by tremors.	Brain, all toes, whole spine, all glands, liver, diaphragm, chest/lung
Tic douloureux	Trigeminal neuralgia: a painful disorder of the trigeminal nerve characterized by severe pain in the face and forehead.	Neck, cervicals, parathyroids, diaphragm
Tremors	An involuntary trembling of the body or limbs.	Brain, all toes, whole spine, diaphragm
Vertigo	Dizziness: a sensation of rotation or movement.	Ear reflex, cervicals, neck, all toes

DISORDERS OF THE MUSCULAR SYSTEM

DISORDER	DESCRIPTION	REFLEX AREAS TO WORK
Cramps (feet, legs, etc.)	A prolonged spasm and pain in a muscle.	Parathyroids, adrenals, lower spine, pelvic area, hip/sciatic, knee/leg
Myasthenia gravis	Great muscular weakness without atrophy of the muscles.	Parathyroids, adrenals, brain, whole spine, neck, chest/lung, diaphragm
Ruptured disk	Rupture of a disc or pad of cartilage between the vertebrae, sometimes called a "slipped disc".	Reflex to affected area, diaphragm
Spasm (see cramps)	A sudden, involuntary contraction of a muscle.	Parathyroids, adrenals, lower spine, pelvic area, hip/sciatic, knee/leg
Sprain	Excessive stretching of the ligaments of a joint capsule.	Reflex to affected area, referral area to affected area
Strain	Excessive stretching of the ligaments of a joint capsule.	Reflex to affected area, referral area to affected area

For a detailed listing of all disorders, see System Disorders at the back of this book.

Chapter 6

THE CARDIOVASCULAR SYSTEM

"For the life of the flesh is in the blood . . . "

Leviticus 17:11

THE CARDIOVASCULAR SYSTEM

Pumping vital nutrients and oxygen to all of the tissues of the body and in turn, carrying away their waste products, including carbon dioxide, is the primary task of that magnificent muscle . . . the heart. It causes blood to circulate through a system of arteries, capillaries and veins.

THE HEART

The heart, the body's most powerful muscle, is a hollow, muscular organ about the size of your clenched fist and it pumps almost 5 liters of blood a minute while you are resting and about 35 liters of blood during exercise.

Putting it another way, the heart's pumping action circulates about 2000 gallons (7570 liters) of blood through an estimated 70,000 miles (112,630 kilometers) of blood vessels every 24 hours.

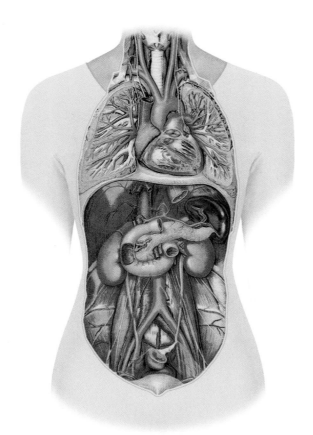

Figure 6.1
The cardiovascular system

THE CARDIOVASCULAR SYSTEM (Figure 6.1)

The heart is located in an oblique position within the thoracic cavity; one third of it is situated on the right side of the midline while the remaining two thirds are to the left. It is composed of 4 distinct compartments: the left and right atria and the left and right ventricles. The pumping cycle consists of a contraction (called systole) and resting/filling stage (called diastole). The right side of the heart receives blood from the veins collected throughout the body and pumps that blood to the lungs to exchange the carbon dioxide waste for fresh oxygen. The left side of the heart receives the oxygen-filled blood and pumps it back into circulation.

This hardest of working muscles must, of course, be enriched and fed with its own blood at all times. (The brain is the only other organ in the human body which actually needs more blood and oxygen than the heart itself.) As a matter of fact, it is estimated that the heart keeps about 5% of all of the blood it pumps. This blood is fed into the heart muscle fibers by the coronary arteries which surround the outside of the heart. It is here, in the coronary arteries, where a build up of a certain type of cholesterol in one of these main arteries can stop the flow of blood to the heart muscle, leading to what is called a myocardial infarction: the death of heart muscle tissue . . . we know this situation as a heart attack.

LUNG/OXYGEN EXCHANGE

The blood is carried to the lungs by the pulmonary artery. In the lungs, and within the tiny capillaries, the blood trades carbon dioxide for fresh new oxygen. The pulmonary veins then carry the blood back to the left atrium of the heart where it begins its journey to the parts of the body. (**See Figure 6.2**)

PULSE

The beat of the heart causes surges of blood through the arteries, not in a steady flow, but in waves of pressure. These waves travel through the arteries. When you place your finger over an artery, you can feel the beat or the surge of pressure . . . called the arterial pulse or simply pulse.

To the trained Reflexologist whose concern is to keep the bodily systems in balance, the Cardiovascular System is extremely important.

The Reflexologist works these reflexes almost as second nature, since this type of preventive therapy can assure the other systems an adequate supply of those nutrients necessary for life. Many circulatory problems are helped by working all the reflexes of the feet.

Elsewhere in this book, I have made mention of the debilitating effects of stress and tension on the human body. This is nowhere more evident than in the Cardiovascular System . . . that essential and intricate lifeline to the organs and cells. Stress and tension act as a tourniquet on this system since tense muscles tighten over the blood vessels and shut off the supply of nutrients and that ever-so-important oxygen.

Since one of the basic advantages of Reflexology is in the improvement of circulation, you can easily see that working the heart reflex is an excellent preventive measure for heart

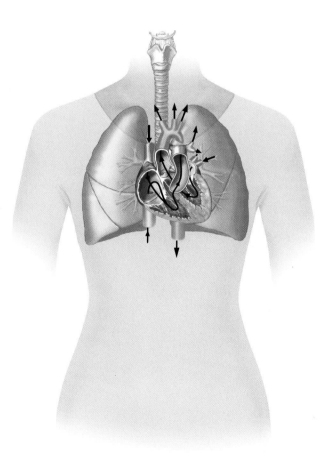

Figure 6.2
Lung/oxygen exchange

problems. I cannot stress too often, any reflex area when worked correctly, will automatically improve circulation to that part of the body.

Unfortunately, with the circulatory system there is no "x" marks the spot like the other reflex areas on the foot. And this is a logical conclusion since blood is circulated to all parts of the body. Therefore, you must work all the reflexes of the foot.

Since circulation is only as good as the pump keeping it moving, you should also be aware of the part exercise and diet play in keeping a preventive program of Reflexology.

Exercise on a regular basis . . . a brisk walk of a mile or two a day, a climb up several flights of stairs, jumping on a mini-trampoline, or more strenuous activities all help keep the heart strong and the blood circulating normally.

As far as diet is concerned, most knowledgeable people know that extra pounds mean extra work for the heart.

When you consider that it has been estimated that every pound of excess fat contains about 20 miles of capillaries for blood to be pumped through, you have some small idea of why diet is important to a healthy heart.

Besides the heart itself, and the arteries and veins which play such an important role in this system, there are other vital areas I will be discussing and with which you should become familiar.

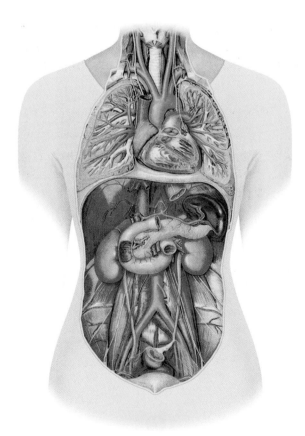

Figure 6.3
The cardiovascular system

Think of the kidneys and how they are affected by high blood pressure. Specifically the liver, the lungs, the portal and renal arteries, all of these must be considered when discussing the Cardiovascular System. Now would be a good time to study **Figure 6.3** which delineates this system and related organs.

ASSOCIATIVE HEART DISORDERS

You should also be familiar with the following associative heart disorder terms:

Angina pectoris – due to an inadequate supply of blood to the muscle tissue of the heart. Generally, the result of a spasm of the arteries feeding the heart or a clogged condition of these arteries.

Aneurysm – dilation of the wall of an artery forming a sac – much like a weak spot on an inner tube.

Arrhythmia – abnormal irregular heart beat.

Arteriosclerosis – Hardening of the arteries caused by a thickening in the layers of the artery wall. Do not confuse this with . . .

Atherosclerosis – this is one sort of arteriosclerosis where fatty deposits accumulate in the inside of an artery – much like lime deposits in the pipes of your water system at home.

Coronary occlusion – obstruction which interferes with the flow of blood through an artery in the heart. This may result in angina pectoris, myocardial infarction or arrhythmia. It can be caused by a clot or arteriosclerosis.

High blood pressure – (*Hypertension*) – a continuous elevation in blood pressure. It is the pressure which blood exerts within the blood vessels. Since the heart is a pump, it alternates between contraction and relaxation. The contraction phase is called systole, the relaxation phase is known as diastole. Blood pressure is commonly referred to as two numbers. The *systole* number refers to the pressure of the heart at work; the lower *diastole* number is the pressure while the heart relaxes. The lower figure is the more important one . . . it tells how much your heart is getting to rest. High blood pressure is due primarily to a spasm of the muscles of the arteries, but may also be brought on by arteriosclerosis. Some of the effects of hypertension are: cardiac hypertrophy, with eventual cardiac failure; further hardening of the arteries (*arteriosclerosis*); possible rupture of blood vessels, especially in the brain (*cerebral hemorrhage, "apoplexy"*); kidney dysfunction due to degenerative changes in renal vessels and visual dysfunction due to blood vessel change in the eyes or brain. There are two types of arterial hypertension: **primary** or **essential**, in which the hypertension is not preceded by kidney disorders or other pathologic conditions, and **renal** hypertension, which accompanies Bright's disease (*nephritis*) and is initiated by renal damage or malfunctioning.

Phlebitis –- inflammation of a vein and can be associated with a blood clot in a vein. Usually occurs in the lower extremities.

Varicose veins – swollen, knotted veins usually in the legs. They happen when the walls of the veins become weak and blood cannot be returned properly to the heart. Blood tends to stagnate in the vein and can lead to phlebitis.

Cardiac arrhythmia – changes in the rhythm of the cardiac contractions caused by disturbances of the electrical activity within the heart muscle.

Coronary artery disease (CAD) –- narrowing or occlusion of the coronary arteries or any of their branches.

Myocardial infarction – damage to a portion of the cardiac muscles as a result of an occlusion of one of the coronary arteries.

Rheumatic valvular disease – damage to a heart valve caused by rheumatic fever.

WORKING THE REFLEXES FOR THE CARDIOVASCULAR SYSTEM

The Heart Area – Work the heart reflex across the metatarsals of the left foot above the diaphragm guideline up to the base of the toes. Generally, the most sensitive area is between the 1st and the 2nd toes. (**See Figures 6.4a, 6.4b**). Work all the way across the foot to the shoulder reflex area on both the dorsal and the plantar surfaces of the foot. Work the same as described for the lungs. Work the left shoulder reflex when working for heart conditions since many people have some discomfort in the shoulder and arm when they have heart problems. Do not forget the nerve supply going to the heart . . . the vagus nerve in that area. Work the cervical and thoracic vertebrae reflexes as well.

A good helper area for some heart conditions would be the adrenal gland reflexes as adrenaline is often given to people who have heart attacks.

Hypertension – Be sure to work the diaphragm reflex in all cases of hypertension. (**See Chapter 4** for more details on working the diaphragm.)

Blood clots – Nature usually takes care of a blood clot by eventually dissolving or absorbing it. Reflexology can help nature dissolve the clot faster simply by working the referral area to the clot area which naturally helps to absorb or dissolve it. We do not work directly on the blood clot itself.

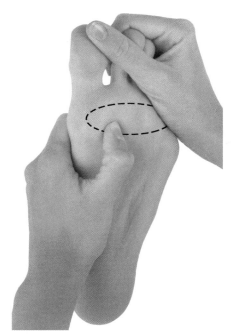

Figure 6.4a

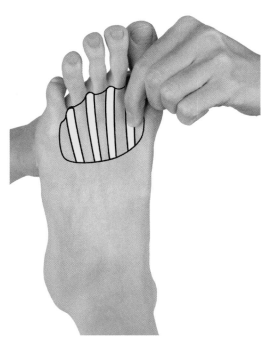

Figure 6.4b

Phlebitis – Usually found in the leg; work the corresponding area on the arm if the phlebitis is in the leg.

Varicose veins – Work the colon reflex and the corresponding areas of the arm.

Stroke – In a stroke, we know that a blood vessel ruptures or a clot in the brain has already occurred, and the damage has been done. You must work the brain reflex in order to help the brain repair itself. It is important to remember, if the paralysis is on the **right side of the body**, it indicates damage to the **opposite** hemisphere of the brain . . . therefore, work the brain reflex (tip of the great toe) on the left foot. (**See Figure 6.5**) This is important to remember when working for a stroke. (**See Chapter 5**, *Nervous System* for working the brain).

Always work the opposite side:

If a stroke is evident on the left side, work the tip of the right great toe and all the small toes.

If a stroke is evident on the right side, work the tip of the left great toe and all the small toes.

Now, let's take a specific look at some particular disorders and corresponding reflex areas to work.

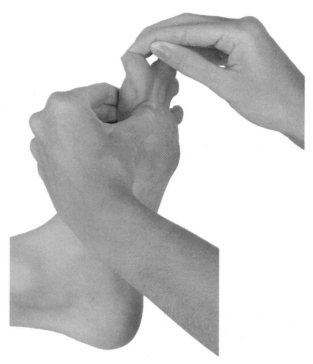

Figure 6.5
Working the brain reflex

DISORDERS OF THE CARDIOVASCULAR SYSTEM

DISORDER	DESCRIPTION	REFLEX AREAS TO WORK
Angina Pectoris	Severe thoracic pain which tends to radiate from the region of the heart to the shoulder and down the left arm. It is accompanied by a feeling of suffocation, which is due to an inadequate supply of blood to the myocardium of the heart; generally the result of coronary spasm or thrombosis.	Chest/lung/ heart, cervicals, thoracics, adrenals, diaphragm, sigmoid colon
Arteriosclerosis	"Hardening" of the arteries is a condition in which there is thickening and loss of elasticity of the layers of the artery wall. Arteriosclerosis is common in advanced age.	All glands: esp. pancreas and thyroid, liver, work entire foot
Atherosclerosis	A type of arteriosclerosis in which fatty deposits accumulate in the artery.	All glands: esp. pancreas and thyroid, liver, work entire foot
Coronary Occlusion	Obstruction of, or interference with the flow of blood through an artery owing to either narrowing of the lumen of the vessels from arteriosclerosis or presence of a thrombus or embolus. The deprivation of oxygen and accumulation of metabolic substances stimulate the pain endings of afferent nerves, giving rise to agonizing chest pains (angina pectoris). Attacks are usually precipitated by muscular exertion or emotional excitement.	Chest/lung/heart, cervicals, thoracics, adrenals, diaphragm, sigmoid colon
High Cholesterol	May be a contributing factor in heart and circulatory diseases, particularly in the formation of fatty deposits in the arteries.	Thyroid, liver
Hypertension (High Blood Pressure)	A condition in which the blood pressure is persistently *above* that which is normal for a given age level.	Diaphragm, kidneys, pituitary, adrenals, thyroid
Hypotension (Low Blood Pressure)	A condition in which the blood pressure is persistently *below* that which is normal for a given age level.	Adrenals, pituitary, thyroid

DISORDER	DESCRIPTION	REFLEX AREAS TO WORK
Phlebitis	Inflammation of a vein, usually accompanied by formation of pus. It frequently leads to the formation of a thrombus within a vein (thrombophlebitis) which may break loose and result in the distribution of infective emboli to other parts of the body. Phlebitis occurs most commonly in the veins of the lower extremities, often following long confinement in bed, abdominal operations, or childbirth.	Referral area: arm, adrenals, colon, liver, gallbladder
Stroke	Rupture or blockage of a blood vessel in the brain; results in loss of consciousness, paralysis or other symptoms of brain damage.	Tip of great toe (opposite side from paralysis), small toes, reflexes to affected areas
Tachycardia	Excessive rapidity of heart beat. In paroxysmal tachycardia the heart begins suddenly to beat at an abnormally high rate, as fast as 150 or more beats per minute.	Chest/lung/heart, thyroid, adrenal, cervicals, thoracics
Varicose Veins	Swollen, knotted, and tortuous veins, most commonly seen in the lower extremities. They are brought on by weakening of the walls of the veins or interference with venous return. Blood tends to stagnate in the vessels, and valves become incompetent.	Referral area: arm, adrenals, colon, liver, gallbladder

For a detailed listing of all disorders, see Systems Disorders at the back of this book.

Chapter 7

THE LYMPHATIC SYSTEM

*"Know ye not that your body is the temple
of the Holy Spirit, which is in you, which ye
have of God, and ye are not your own?"*

1 Cor. 6-19

THE LYMPHATIC SYSTEM

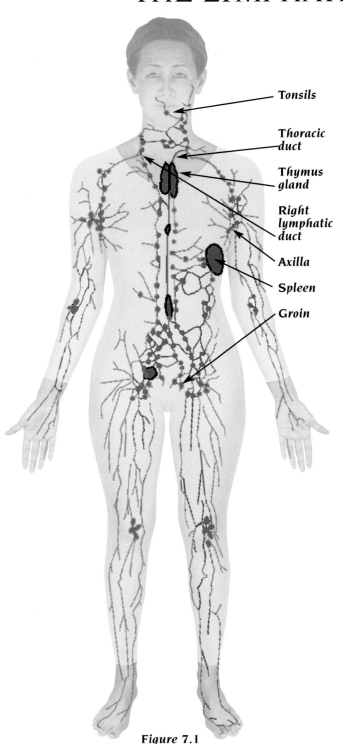

Tonsils

Thoracic
duct

Thymus
gland

Right
lymphatic
duct

Axilla

Spleen

Groin

Figure 7.1
The lymphatic system

The Lymphatic System forms a network of vessels throughout the body almost like the blood vessels, only the Lymphatic System's vessels contain more valves. The system is usually thought of as being part of the Cardiovascular System. (**See Figure 7.1**)

Lymph is derived from the blood plasma and is a colorless fluid rich in cells. As the plasma circulates throughout the body, some of it seeps through the capillary walls as well as from other blood vessels; this leaked fluid is lymph. One of its primary functions is to supply a fluid environment between the cells and the tissues . . . it actually *bathes* them. To keep this fluid circulating, there is a drainage field within the body which ends up in so called collecting stations, or nodes. The lymph carries dead and worn out cells as well as harmful bacteria and viruses along with it to these collecting stations . . . there are several hundred of these nodes throughout the body. The nodes can be thought of as outposts for defense against the harmful bacteria, virus, etc., approaching the interior of the body. Many of us are familiar with the swollen nodes in the groin, breast, neck and armpit . . . the most notable of these nodes.

THE SPLEEN

The largest mass of lymphatic tissue in the body is the spleen whose main function is the production of protective antibodies. The spleen also acts as a blood filter, since it has the responsibility of ridding the body of old red blood cells and bacteria. Iron storage is another of its functions. This is important since it helps to produce hemoglobin from old red blood cells . . . quite important to the Reflexologist when working on anemia and related dysfunctions.

THE TONSILS

The tonsils are also included in this system since they are composed of masses of lymphoid tissue. The only known functions of the tonsils are the formation of antibodies and lymphocytes as well as serving as special filters.

THE THYMUS GLAND

The thymus gland is a lymphatic organ and part of the Endocrine System, located just in front of, and above, the heart. This organ grows rather rapidly from birth to puberty and then begins to diminish in size. As a matter of fact, an adult lives quite comfortably without one. Since it does play an important part in producing antibodies and controlling the body's immune system during childhood, it represents a very important reflex to work in children.

WORKING THE REFLEXES FOR THE LYMPHATIC SYSTEM

Since the Lymphatic System is closely allied with the Cardiovascular System, it is not too surprising to learn that every area that is worked on the feet indirectly helps the Lymphatic System. This is not to say that the system should be ignored, not in the least. There are several vital areas which we must always consider when working this system.

GROIN REFLEX

The first of these key areas is referred to as the groin reflex. Since the groin is located on the body where the upper leg is joined to the torso, the corresponding reflex on the foot is where the ankle and the foot meet. This specific reflex represents the location in the body of a large cluster of lymph nodes and where, quite often, there is congestion in these nodes which creates problems for the entire system. Therefore, you should concentrate a great deal of attention and effort on this reflex.

To work the groin reflex, remember to keep the foot back. Pulling the foot forward is often a natural thing since you are trying to see exactly where you are working. It is better to resist that temptation because you will not get into the reflex effectively.

Keeping the foot back, place the thumb on the bottom of the heel for leverage,

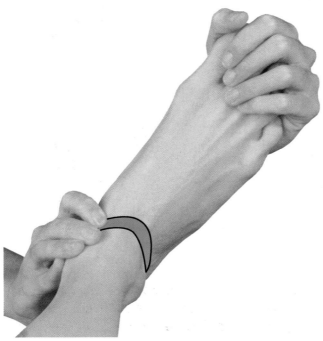

Figure 7.2a
Working the groin reflex medial to lateral

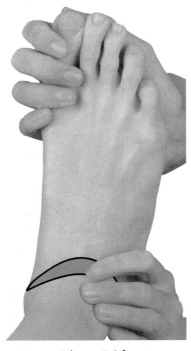

Figure 7.2b
Working the groin reflex lateral to medial

then place the index finger of the right hand just below the anklebone, then walk it in a forward motion, using 20 to 25 small bites, ending just below the opposite anklebone. Repeat the process with the alternate hand. (**See Figures 7.2a, 7.2b**) Work this region several times in this manner with both hands. You will notice that the fingers get into the reflex area a lot easier. It is preferable to use the fingers in order not to tire the thumb which will be used for the more difficult tasks.

There are also relaxing techniques, the Ankle Stretch "Over" and Ankle Stretch "Under", which are appropriate to use here. (**See Figures 7.3, 7.4**) These, too, can be done with either hand. Of course, one hand may seem a little easier for you than the other, but remember that this process can and should be repeated on both feet. This is very important!

CHEST, LUNG, BREAST REFLEX AREA

The next important area in discussing the Lymphatic System is the lungs, chest and breast reflex.

There are large lymphatic networks in the breast and in the arm pits, so this region is very important to the Reflexologist. This particular reflex is located from the diaphragm guideline to the base of the toes . . . from the small toe to the great toe on both the dorsum and the plantar surface of both feet.

I have found that it is much easier to work these reflexes on the dorsum of the foot since the heavy padding on the plantar surface of the foot makes it difficult to work. This, of course, does not mean that you cannot work the plantar surface of the foot, but experience has indicated that the dorsum of the foot is much more effective in working this specific reflex.

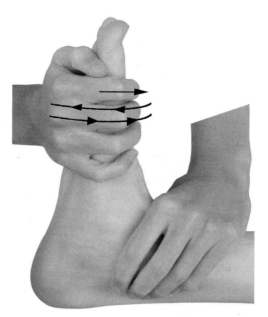

Figure 7.3
Ankle stretch "over" technique

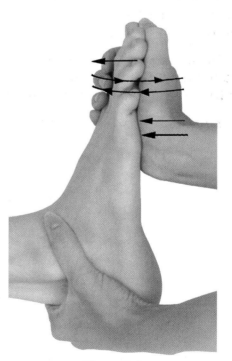

Figure 7.4
Ankle stretch "under" technique

This particular region will be worked using the fingers on the dorsum of each foot; the thumb is used for working on the plantar surface. Use both hands remembering to keep the foot in an upright position. Again, I must advise you **not** to pull the foot towards you just so you can see the area you are working.

83

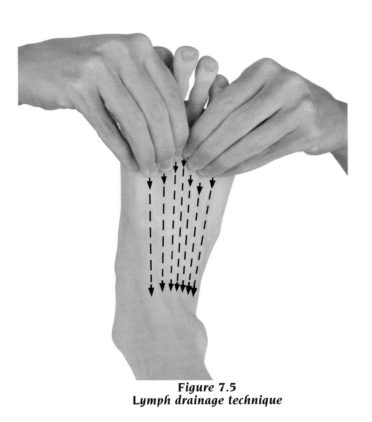

Figure 7.5
Lymph drainage technique

Start working either from the little toe side or the great toe side of the foot. Use 10 to 15 small bites down the side of all 4 grooves. It is important to work the foot in both directions using the hands separately. This enables you to contact both sides of the metatarsal grooves. (**See Figure 6.4b**)

Actually,   when   working between the 1st and 2nd toe just below the base of the toe you will be working what is referred to as the lymph drainage reflex area. This represents the area where the thoracic duct and the drainage for the Lymphatic System are located. Anatomically, it is where the subclavian and the jugular veins come together deep in the base of the neck on both sides . . . so naturally, this is the reflex area for lymphatic drainage.

Another useful technique to use for lymph edema is the lymphatic drainage technique. Place both thumbs on the diaphragm reflex and push the foot back and straight. Place the fingers of both hands at the base of the toes on the dorsal side of the foot, squeeze, push the fingers forward while walking down the entire dorsal surface until you reach the ankle joint.   Make sure the fingers are kept straight as only the 1st joint of the fingers should be bending simultaneously while walking. Lift the hands and repeat the process several times. (**See Figure 7.5**)

In all cases, this region across the dorsal surface of the foot represents the reflexes to the lung, chest and breast, and is extremely helpful for assisting the Lymphatic System.

Another important area to work is the shoulder reflex since many lymph nodes are located in that region. (The detailed discussion on working this reflex area will be discussed in **Chapter 9.**)

TONSILS AND ADENOIDS

An additional and rather important area of the Lymphatic System is the tonsil/adenoid reflex. These reflexes will be located on the great toe since that is the reflex to the neck and head. Be sure to work the neck reflex and **not** the area where the toe is joined onto the foot. Anatomically, the tonsils/adenoids are located in the upper region of the neck, consequently, the reflex will be located approximately one third of the way up the great toe from its base.

Let the index finger work around the dorsum of the great toe from the medial edge to the lateral edge. The right thumb will work from the medial edge to the lateral edge on the plantar surface of the toe. You can then come back on both the dorsum and the plantar surfaces in the opposite direction with the alternate thumb and finger. This reflex will be found on both feet.

The helper area for the tonsils and adenoids will be the small toes.

One thing to remember: when working the toes, use 6 to 10 small bites down each path. The toes **are** small and usually require changing hands and working them in both directions with each thumb.   As I have stated, there are many reflexes which require approaching the reflex from different angles in order to locate them.

THYMUS GLAND

Another part of the Lymphatic System is the thymus gland which is located below the thyroid gland, beneath the sternum (breastbone) and alongside the upper thoracic vertebrae.

Work this reflex with the basic thumb technique from the diaphragm reflex to the base of the great toe along the spinal reflex. This reflex is important for children.

Now, let's take a specific look at some particular disorders and corresponding reflex areas to work.

DISORDERS OF THE LYMPHATIC SYSTEM

DISORDER	DESCRIPTION	REFLEX AREAS TO WORK
Ankles (swollen)	The presence of abnormally large amounts of fluid in the tissue spaces around the ankles.	Adrenals, kidneys, Lymphatic System, referral area: wrist
Breast Lumps	Most lumps of the breasts are benign and are usually infected lymph nodes.	Chest/lung, Lymphatic System, pituitary
Edema	The presence of abnormally large amounts of fluid in the intercellular tissue spaces of the body.	Adrenals, pituitary, Lymphatic System, kidneys
Fluid Retention	Same as edema.	Adrenals, pituitary, Lymphatic System, kidneys
Infections	An invasion of the body by bacteria.	Region or area affected, adrenals, Lymphatic System, spleen, liver, kidneys
Leukemia	A disease of the blood-forming organs, characterized by an increase in the number of leukocytes and their precursors in the blood, causing enlargement and proliferation of the lymphoid tissue of the spleen, lymphatic glands and bone marrow.	Spleen, Lymphatic System, liver, all glands
Sore Throat	Inflammation of the throat and tonsils.	Throat/neck, all toes, cervicals, Lymphatic System, adrenals
Tonsillitis	Inflammation of the tonsils, a small mass of lymphoid tissue.	All toes, Lymphatic System, adrenals, cervicals, neck

For a detailed listing of all disorders, see Systems Disorders at the back of this book.

THE SENSE ORGANS

". . . For I am fearfully and wonderfully made . . ."

Psalms 139:14

THE SENSE ORGANS

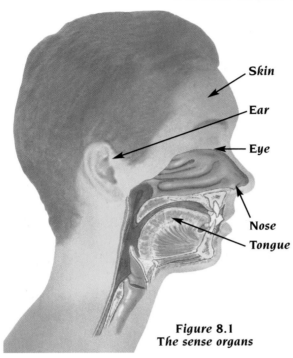

Skin

Ear

Eye

Nose

Tongue

Figure 8.1
The sense organs

This special system includes those Sense Organs which are used to make the body aware of its environment both outside and inside of the body. (**See Figure 8.1**)

These sense organs include:

- **The Skin** – *Touch, Pain, Pressure and Temperature*
- **The Eyes** – *Vision*
- **The Ears** – *Hearing and Equilibrium*
- **The Nose** – *Smell*
- **The Tongue** – *Taste*

These Sense Organs are commonly classified according to the type of information the body receives.

- There are sensations which give information about the external environment. They include touch, pressure, temperature, pain, hearing, sight and smell.

- The Sense Organs which give information about the internal environment. They include pain, taste, fatigue, hunger, thirst, nausea, etc.

- The Sense Organs which give information about the body's position and movement – the sense of equilibrium (the inner ear) and proprioceptors (sensory nerve terminals) from the muscles, tendons and joints indicate their position in relation to the body as a whole.

THE SKIN

The skin is much more than just a *wrapper* keeping the body together. It produces one important vitamin, vitamin D. It is also responsible for helping to regulate body temperature through a complex *thermostat*. The skin is also the barrier which bacteria must penetrate before causing damage to the organs and systems of the body. The skin contains millions of sweat glands which help to regulate the body's temperature as well as keep the delicate balance between salt and water. The skin is an important excretory organ serving in the healthy person to excrete about 500cc of water as it regulates body temperature. The complex structure of the network of nerves in the skin is awesome . . . many of which act as receptor organs for the sense of touch and pain, as well as cold and heat.

The Olfactory Sense (*sense of smell*). The nose is an organ which not only is used for the sense of smell, but is also used to *clean* and condition the air before it enters the lungs . . . warming the air on a cold day, freeing it of particles and irritants and giving it the proper moisture. The nose is capable of recognizing 4,000 different scents through the utilization of special receptor cells on the roof of each nasal cavity.

The Gustatory Sense (*sensations of taste*). Taste is accomplished through the use of receptors or *taste buds* on the tongue itself. The tongue not only aids in the sensation of taste, but is also essential to speech and to aid in swallowing food. But taste is of primary importance to the tongue which automatically recognizes four primary groups: sour, salty, bitter and sweet. Sweet taste buds are located mainly on the tip of the tongue, bitter at the back, salty at the sides and tip, and sour at the sides.

The Visual Sense (*sense of sight*). The visual organ of sight, the eye, is perhaps one of the most complex organs in the body. Millions of nerve connections can handle over a million simultaneous messages. When looking at a cut-away drawing of the eye, you can easily compare it to a camera. The *window* of the eye, the cornea actually bends the light rays; the pupil which is an adjustable iris allows only the right amount of light to enter. The lens adjusts the focus by a series of muscles which flatten it for distance vision and allow it to thicken for near vision. The lens is surrounded by fluid. Light passing through the fluid and the lens is focused on the retina which covers most of the interior of the eye. Millions of light sensitive receptor cells are contained in the retina. . . some shaped like rods, for black and white vision, others are cones for sharp color vision. All impulses received at the retina are carried to the brain through the optic nerve.

SPECIFIC DISORDERS OF THE EYE INCLUDE:

Myopia, or nearsightedness, a condition in which light rays come to a focus slightly in front of the retina.

Hyperopia, or farsightedness, a condition in which the light rays come to a focus slightly behind the retina.

Astigmatism is due to irregularities in the curvature of the cornea or of the lens.

Cataract is a loss of transparency of the crystalline lens.

Glaucoma is caused when intraocular pressure increases due to an overproduction of intraocular fluid, or the drainage canal becomes blocked.

Tunnel Vision is when the field of vision becomes narrowed.

Conjunctivitis is an inflammation of the membrane which lines the eyelids.

Detached Retina is a complete or partial separation of the retina from the inner layers of the eye (choroid).

Sties are a bacterial infection of one of the sebaceous glands of the eyelid.

HEARING AND EQUILIBRIUM

The ear is a complex organ, not only of hearing, but also of balance. It is divided into: 1) the external ear, 2) the middle ear and 3) the inner ear. (**See Figure 8.2**)

The outer ear gathers sound much like a disk antenna one sees scanning the skies during an orbital flight. It picks up the sound, sends it down the one inch canal to the ear drum or tympanic membrane. The ear drum is set in motion by the sound waves hitting it. This vibratory motion is magnified about 22 times its original force through a series of three small bones called the anvil, hammer and stirrup (since they actually resemble an *anvil, hammer* and *stirrup*). From here, the sound goes to the inner ear.

The inner ear is made up of a complicated series of canals which contain sensory receptors. The main component is called the cochlea because it looks like a snail's shell; it is made up of a spiral canal which is filled with microscopic nerve cells . . . each one *pre-tuned* to a particular vibration. When a nerve cell (actually very thin hair cells) vibrates, it produces a minute electrical current which goes into the acoustic nerve . . . the nerve of hearing, called the auditory nerve. This particular nerve sends the impulse to the brain for translation.

The inner ear has another very important function to perform . . . that of equilibrium or *balance*. This is accomplished by a unique arrangement of structures called the semi-circular ducts filled with a fluid called endolymph. One of the canals reads up and down motion, one forward motion and the third one lateral or side motion.

Motion of the body causes the fluid in one of the canals to be displaced and tiny hair cells detect the fact and send it to the brain which orders the body to *get back in balance*.

Pressure within the middle ear cavity is equalized with external pressure through the eustachian tube. The eustachian tube runs from the middle ear to the pharynx and provides an air passage which equalizes pressure on both sides of the eardrum. The middle ear is often the site of infection, particu-

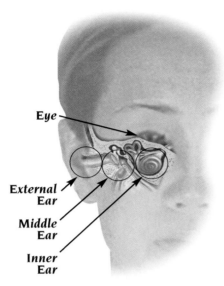

Eye

External Ear

Middle Ear

Inner Ear

Figure 8.2
The eye and ear

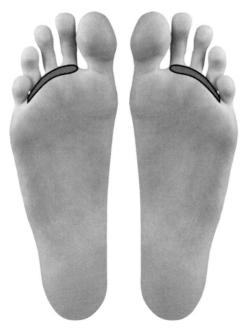

Figure 8.3
Eye and ear reflex

larly in children. This infection of the middle ear is called Otitis Media and can lead to serious difficulties. The middle ear is directly connected with the mastoid air cells contained in the mastoid bone just behind the outer ears.

WORKING THE REFLEXES
FOR THE SENSE ORGANS

EYE AND EAR REFLEX

These important reflexes are located in the same area on both feet . . . at the base of the small toes. (**See Figure 8.3**)

When working this reflex area, you will alternate the right hand with the left hand.

The eye and ear reflex is a rather difficult one in that the technique I recommend is a bit different from those used for other reflexes.

Start on the right foot with the right hand as the working hand. The fingers of the left hand (holding hand) are placed on the dorsum of the foot opposite the thumb. The thumb is placed on the diaphragm guideline and holds the foot firmly. Note how the thumb is flat against the metatarsal area along the plantar surface of the foot. (**See Figure 8.4a, 8.4b**)

Place the right thumb of the working hand on the ridge making sure to use the **lateral** edge of the thumb. (**See Chapter 4**) The ridge is formed where the base of the small toes meet the metatarsal padding. I have coined the phrase *walking the ridge* especially for this maneuver since it seems to adequately describe the working regi-

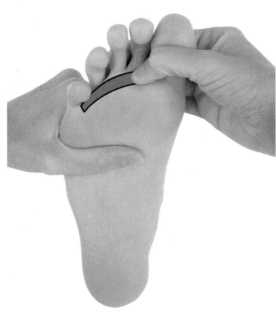

Figure 8.4a
Working the eye and ear reflex
medial to lateral

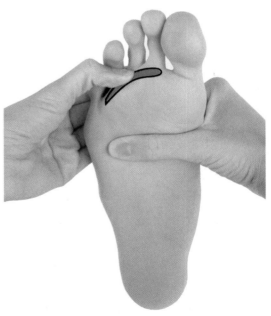

Figure 8.4b
Working the eye and ear reflex
lateral to medial

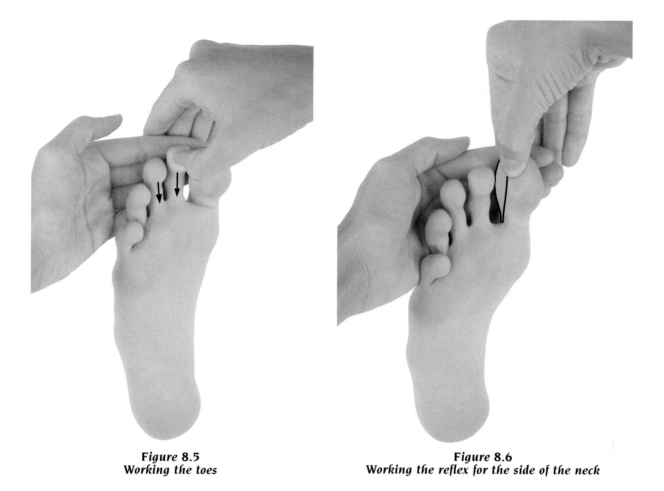

Figure 8.5
Working the toes

Figure 8.6
Working the reflex for the side of the neck

men. The thumb will walk from medial to lateral in a forward motion across this ridge starting at the base of the second toe and continuing to the lateral edge of the foot. I must stress the use of the **lateral** edge of the thumb because using the medial edge is less effective.

The walking motion must be one in which the thumb walks all the way across the base of the small toes, is picked up, comes back and starts over . . . with the pressure of the thumb exerted downward toward the heel.

To gain maximum effectiveness, I recommend a continuous walking with one hand, repeating several times, then change hands and walk in the opposite direction several times. Repeat this process on the left foot, starting with the left thumb.

Important pointers when working the eye and ear reflex:

On a heavy fleshy, or callused foot apply a greater degree of pressure downward with the thumb . . . but be careful not to squeeze the area with the holding hand. This causes the padding to push up toward the base of the toes and you will have a difficult time finding the reflex area.

Be careful of any broken skin between the toes.

It should be reiterated here that the eye and ear reflexes actually overlap one another. Remember, the "packed suitcase" analogy made in **Chapter 2**, the ear lies anatomically behind the eye. Frequently, I am asked why we don't just work the great toes for the eye and ear reflexes since they have all 5 zones in each. The answer to that is based upon years of experience in that it is extremely difficult to find these reflexes in the great toe since they would be comparatively smaller. Consequently, I have found that the best results can be obtained by working the base of the toes and the shafts of the 2nd and 3rd toes. (**See Figure 8.5**)

HELPER AREAS FOR THE EYES AND EARS

Now, I would like to discuss some valuable helper areas for the eye and ear reflex.

The side of the neck reflex can be found on the lateral edge of the great toes. (**See Figure 8.6**) Work this area from the tip of the great toe to its base and work the cervical reflex on the medial side of the great toe. These reflexes are very important for helping the nerve and blood supply to the eyes and ears.

Another effective helper area I have found is the throat region where the great toes are joined onto the feet. This region includes the area between the base of the toe and the "ball" of the toe. This area can be effective for such maladies as ear problems (ear infections), enlarged tonsils, sluggish lymph glands and mastoids. The reflex for the eustachian tube is also found in this area. Work the entire region from where the great toe is joined to the foot right up to the 1st joint of the great toe and around the toe itself.

As a matter of fact, I have found, because of the zone lines, working all the toes is very helpful for many eye problems as well as the sinuses. They often affect one another.

Ears can also be helped by working these same areas since they are in the same zones.

Another helper area for the eyes is the kidney reflex. The kidneys are in zones 2 and 3 in the body, the same zones as the eyes. Now, we know that there is no anatomical connection between the eye and the kidney, but do you remember grandmother saying *"dark circles under the eyes indicate kidney problems"*?

Well, through my many years with Reflexology, I can appreciate that old saying, for I have found that working the kidney reflex often is very helpful for some eye problems.

By working the eye reflexes I won't promise that you are going to be able to throw your eye glasses away! What I am saying is that if the eyes are growing weaker, you may be able to prevent further deterioration and not have to change your eye glasses as often.

SKIN REFLEXES

The body is surrounded by skin! Everything we do, every reflex that is worked can help some part of our skin. Every organ, every gland, has some indirect effect on our skin.

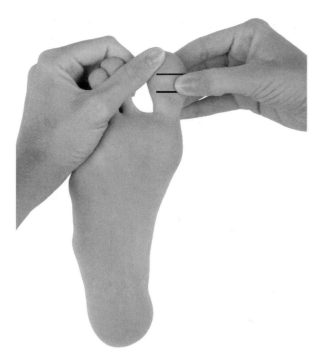

Figure 8.7a
Working for smell and taste
medial to lateral

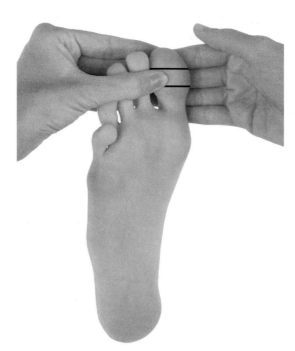

Figure 8.7b
Working for smell and taste
lateral to medial

But I have found some glands are key reflex areas for skin conditions . . . the endocrine glands, the thyroid and the adrenal glands in particular. These are important for such skin conditions as dryness, eczema, psoriasis, hives and some nerve-related cases of shingles.

The kidneys (master chemists of the body) and the liver help to purify the blood and can also have a lot to do with skin conditions. The large intestine also helps skin problems as the skin is the largest excretory organ. Diet also has a great effect on the skin.

SMELL AND TASTE

The sense organs of smell and taste are naturally located in the middle of the head region so we concentrate on working the middle third of the great toe. (**See Figures 8.7a, 8.7b**)

To work this region, use the standard thumb technique in all directions, up, down and across.

Let me interject a personal view here.

In my many travels and in all my seminars, I take the time to preach a small sermon against smoking. The Surgeon General has said it all many times so I only join my small voice with those of the physicians and non-smokers in all areas of the world.

Smoking is destructive . . . it is a habit that can kill you!

As a Reflexologist interested in restoring balance and consequent health, you are going to become acquainted with the effects of smoking.

Smoking destroys smell and taste. People who have stopped this habit almost immediately notice how much better their food tastes . . . and they realize that their sense of smell improves. Nicotine constricts arteries, raises blood pressure, and stimulates the heart to beat harder and faster. Tobacco contains toxic chemicals such as cadmium, radioactive elements, insecticides and tars. Smokers have a much increased incidence of heart disease and lung cancer compared to their non-smoking counterparts.

But . . . why people who want good health continue to puff away is a mystery to me. You should take every opportunity to dissuade your clients from smoking.

In all likelihood, the addictive nature of smoking explains its hold on so many. Chronic cigarette smoking is a good example of drug dependence. Reduction of tension through Reflexology can assist an individual in breaking this pernicious habit.

My sermon is over. I can only reiterate that working around the area of the great toe is very helpful for taste and smell. This is a natural conclusion when you realize that the taste buds are in the tongue area. The mouth and nose reflexes are found in the middle third of the great toe.

The nose, of course, is the organ of smell and also can be the source of discomfort in the form of polyps. The sinus reflexes are helpful to our sense of smell and are also the site of infection. **See Chapter 9** for working the sinus reflexes.

All of these conditions are alleviated by working the entire great toe, throat and head reflex area as well as all the toes.

Now, let's take a specific look at some particular disorders and corresponding reflex areas to work.

DISORDERS OF THE SENSE ORGANS

DISORDER	DESCRIPTION	REFLEX AREAS TO WORK
Acne	A disorder characterized by eruptions or pustules, usually occurring at puberty.	All glands: esp. thyroid and adrenal, liver, kidneys, intestines, diaphragm
Dry Skin	Self descriptive.	Thyroid, adrenals
Eczema	A skin rash characterized by itching, swelling, blistering and scaling of skin.	All glands: esp. adrenal and thyroid, liver, kidneys, intestines, diaphragm
Halitosis	Offensive breath; bad breath.	Stomach, liver, intestines, all toes
Lupus	Tuberculosis of the skin marked by formation of reddish brown eruptions.	All glands, intestines, liver, whole spine, diaphragm
Nasal Polyps	Focal accumulation of edema fluid in the nose, with hyperplasia of the associated mucosa of the nose with thickening of the submucosal connective tissue.	All toes, all glands: esp. pituitary and adrenal
Perspiring hands and feet	Self descriptive.	All glands, kidneys, liver, intestines, diaphragm
Psoriasis	A chronic skin disease marked by red patches covered with silver scales. Cause unknown.	All glands: esp. thyroid and adrenal, liver, kidneys, intestines, diaphragm
Shingles	An acute virus disease characterized by inflammation of spinal ganglia with eruptions along the affected sensory nerve.	Whole spine, all glands, diaphragm
Tongue disorders	Self descriptive.	All toes

For a detailed listing of all disorders, see Systems Disorders at the back of this book.

DISORDERS OF THE SENSE ORGANS – EYE

DISORDER	DESCRIPTION	REFLEX AREAS TO WORK
Cataracts	An opacity of the crystalline eye lens.	Eye reflex, all toes, neck, cervicals, kidneys, pituitary
Glaucoma	A condition of the eye characterized by increased intraocular pressure.	Eye reflex, cervicals, neck, all toes, kidneys
Pink Eye	An inflammation of the conjunctiva – contagious.	Eye reflex, all toes, cervicals, neck, adrenals
Sty	Inflammation of one or more sebaceous glands of the eyelid.	Eye reflex, all toes, cervicals, neck, adrenals

DISORDERS OF THE SENSE ORGANS – EAR

DISORDER	DESCRIPTION	REFLEX AREAS TO WORK
Deafness	Complete or partial loss of ability to hear.	Ear reflex, cervicals, neck, all toes
Dizziness	Vertigo. A sensation of unsteadiness with a feeling of movement within the head.	Ear reflex, cervicals, neck, all toes
Earache (infection)	Inflamed condition of the ear.	Ear reflex, all toes, cervicals, throat/neck (eustachian tube), adrenals
Motion Sickness	Nausea, vomiting and vertigo induced by irregular or rhythmic movements.	Ear reflex, neck, cervicals, diaphragm, stomach
Tinnitus	A ringing or tinkling sound in the ear.	Ear reflex, all toes, cervicals, neck
Vertigo	Balance disturbance, difficulty in maintaining balance.	Ear reflex, cervicals, neck, all toes

For a detailed listing of all disorders, see Systems Disorders at the back of this book.

THE RESPIRATORY SYSTEM

*"The Spirit of God hath made me, and the
breath of the Almighty hath given me life."*

Job 33:4

THE RESPIRATORY SYSTEM

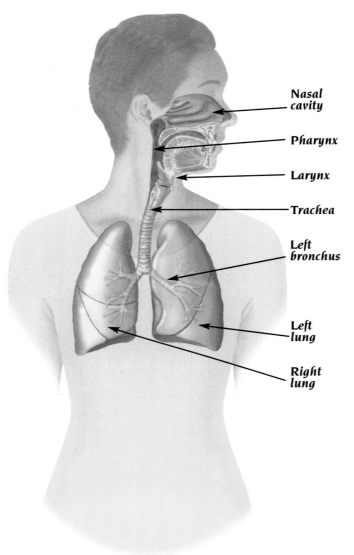

Nasal cavity

Pharynx

Larynx

Trachea

Left bronchus

Left lung

Right lung

Figure 9.1
The respiratory system

The Respiratory System includes: the nose, sinuses, throat region (the pharynx and the larynx), windpipe (trachea), bronchi, lungs and the diaphragm. (**See Figure 9.1**)

The Respiratory System is responsible for the exchange of oxygen and carbon dioxide. . . a life-sustaining process termed *breathing*. It's not such a simple operation once you examine the mechanics of breathing more closely.

Adjacent to the nasal cavity are air spaces called the paranasal sinuses. They contain mucous glands and have cilia which convey the mucus through small channels into the nasal cavity. These sinuses are important particularly in persons suffering from colds, flu and related illnesses and should not be passed over in working the reflexes associated with the respiratory system. The Sinuses are not fully developed until adult life. Air is inhaled through the nose, pharynx, larynx, trachea, right and left bronchi and finally into the alveoli or air sacs in the lung. It is here that the oxygen is exchanged for the waste material, carbon dioxide.

The trachea branches at the back of the throat (pharynx). The top half of the trachea is the larynx or voice box containing the vocal cords. Below this area, the trachea descends to just behind the sternum and branches into the right and left bronchi, then subdivides into the bronchioles and finally the alveoli. Both of the lungs are covered by a thin tissue called the pleura which also lines the inside of the thoracic cavity. The large right lung has three distinct lobes: the left lung has only an upper and lower lobe.

The air reaches its final destination in the lungs through the action of the diaphragm. When the diaphragm contracts, it causes the chest cavity to expand, since the chest cavity is a vacuum, and the lungs hang in this cavity, the enlargement of the vacuum area causes air to be drawn into the lungs. When the diaphragm relaxes, the chest walls return to their original position, thus increasing the pressure, which, in turn, forces the air out of the lungs.

Of particular importance to the Reflexologist are the lungs themselves. Each lung is cone-shaped with its base resting on the diaphragm. The tip of each lung (the apex) extends up into the base of the neck. The entire thoracic cavity is lined with a membrane which completely covers the lungs . . . the pleura. Inflammation of this membrane is known as pleurisy.

Several large structures either enter or leave the lungs, including the bronchi, the pulmonary artery and veins, the bronchial arteries and veins, and the lymphatic vessels.

Let's examine these structures and their functions more closely . . .

The right half of the heart receives the oxygen-poor blood from the veins of the body. This blood enters the heart at the right atrium and then flows down to the right ventricle which pumps the blood to the lungs via the pulmonary artery. In the lungs, the blood passes through tiny capillaries where it picks up oxygen from the alveoli in a chemical *trade off*. This oxygen poor blood carries the carbon dioxide from the cells in the body and *trades* it for oxygen.

In the lungs, the tiny capillaries touch equally small structures called alveoli . . . the smallest air sacs of the lungs. Every breath of air which is taken, goes into the lungs to fill these air sacs. As a matter of fact, it has been estimated that there are anywhere from 300 million to one billion of these air sacs in our lungs. It is here that the important exchange takes place . . . carbon dioxide for oxygen through the one cell thin walls of the capillaries and the alveoli. The carbon dioxide is then expelled (exhaled) from the body while the oxygen is carried in the blood via veins leading away from the lungs to the left atrium of the heart.

It is estimated that the total surface area within the lungs which is exposed to air is about 600 square feet.

SMOKING AND THE LUNGS

The body's air cleaning process begins with the small hairs in the nose, throat and bronchial passages . . . tiny hairs, called cilia, wave back and forth to trap tiny alien particles. What is important to remember here is that cigarette smoking paralyzes this action. Sometimes these cilia, when constantly exposed to cigarette smoke, die. As a result of faulty ciliary function, particles, mucus and other fluids formed within the air passages often find their way into the alveoli . . . those all-important air sacs. When these sacs become plugged, air cannot be exchanged. The heavy cigarette smoker is in danger of actually drowning as in the case of emphysema.

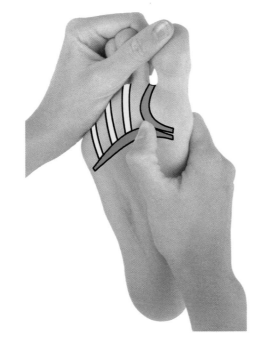

Figure 9.2
Working the lung reflex

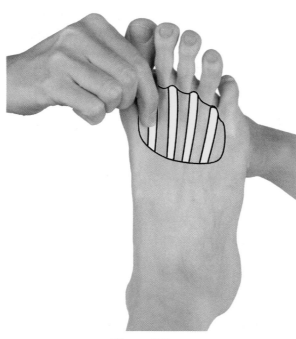

Figure 9.3
Working the lung/breast reflex
(dorsal surface)

WORKING THE REFLEXES FOR THE RESPIRATORY SYSTEM

Working this system is basically working those areas associated with breathing: the lung and chest reflex areas. Actually, some of the reflexes that were described in the Lymphatic System are almost the same as those for the Respiratory System because the breast, chest and lung are in the same area.

LUNG REFLEX

The lung reflex is located from the diaphragm guideline up to the base of the toes and across the entire foot (from the medial to the lateral side) on both the dorsum and the plantar surface of the foot as this represents the entire lung region.

First, work the plantar surface of the foot; this area may be more callused and will need more firmness. When working the area on the plantar surface of the right foot for the lung reflex, use the basic holding position. Tilt the foot slightly outwards and gently spread the toes. Using the right thumb, apply the basic thumb technique, work up the grooves formed by the bones between each toe (**See Figure 9.2**), starting with the groove between the great toe and the 2nd toe . . . remember to separate the great toe and the 2nd toe with the holding hand in order to open the grooves properly. After several passes up this area, proceed with the same technique in the groove between the 2nd and the 3rd toes; then the 3rd and 4th toes; and then the 4th and 5th toes. Change hands and with the left thumb, work back in the opposite direction starting with the groove between the 4th and 5th toes. Repeat this procedure on the left foot, starting with the left thumb.

Work this same area on the dorsal surface of the foot. This area may be very tender and should be worked very gently at first . . . working just to the client's discomfort tolerance.

Start with the right foot using the right hand as the working hand. Place the left fist (holding hand) on the metatarsal padding, push forward to spread the metatarsal bones of the foot, then place the thumb of the working hand on the index finger of the holding hand for leverage (**See Figure 9.3**) and work down the dorsum of the foot with the medial corner of the index finger. Work in the groove between the great toe and the 2nd toe, making sure the fist is pushing the foot back as this will spread the region while working. Line up the 1st knuckle of the fist with the groove you are working, this enables the working finger to line up with that groove. Work this area several times and then move to the following grooves repeating this procedure with each groove. (**See Figure 9.4**) Change hands and repeat this procedure in the opposite direction.

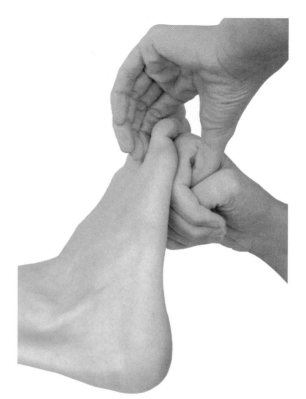

Figure 9.4
The holding hand for working the lung reflex

Another way to work on the dorsum of the right foot is to use the holding hand (left hand) to spread the great toe and the 2nd toe. Hold the foot up straight. The thumb of the working hand (right hand) will be placed on the plantar surface of the foot on the metatarsal padding. The thumb pushes very firmly to spread the area being worked on. The index finger will do the walking in a forward direction on the dorsum of the foot.   After several passes in this groove, move on to the next groove. Work in this manner all the way to the last groove between the 4th and 5th toes. Change hands and repeat the procedure in the opposite direction. Be sure not to pull the foot toward you to see where you are working as this will tighten the surface of the foot and thus prevent contact with the reflexes.

BRONCHIAL TUBE REFLEX

When working the area between the great toe and the 2nd toe on both the dorsal and plantar surfaces you will be working the reflexes to the bronchial tubes that lead to the lungs which are found from the diaphragm guideline to the base of the toes on both the dorsal and plantar surfaces.

DIAPHRAGM REFLEX

The diaphragm is part of the Respiratory System since it is an intricate part of the breathing apparatus as well as being a key reflex for stress and tension.   The diaphragm reflex is found at the distal heads of the metatarsal bones and working this

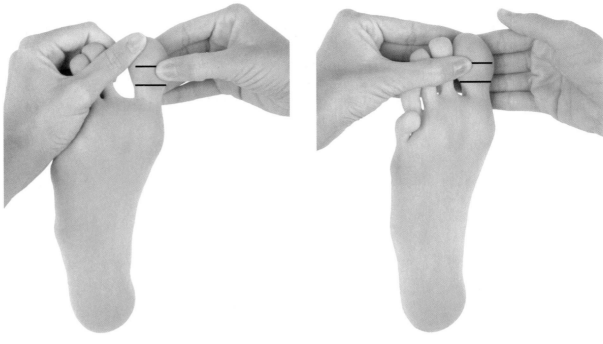

Figure 9.5a
*Working the nose and throat reflex
medial to lateral*

Figure 9.5b
*Working the nose and throat reflex
lateral to medial*

reflex will relieve a lot of lung conditions, including pneumonia, bronchitis, asthma, and emphysema. (**See Chapter 4** for working the diaphragm reflex.)

NOSE AND THROAT REFLEXES

The reflex to the nose will be found in the middle third of the ball of the great toe. (**See Figures 9.5a, 9.5b**) The nose reflex may be helpful for polyps in the nose as well as for adenoids. The throat reflex area will be found on the neck of the great toe below the middle third. This reflex is helpful for sore throats, tonsillitis and eustachian tube problems. (For a detailed analysis of working this reflex, see the Sense Organs **Chapter 8**).

SINUS REFLEXES

The sinus reflexes are found on the balls of all the toes; the great toe having all 5 zones and represents the entire head, while the 4 minor toes on each foot are used for *fine tuning*.

When working this reflex, remember to support and protect the toes at all times. This is important since the toes are sensitive and are the most difficult reflex areas to work and master properly.

Starting on the right foot, use the right hand as the working hand and the left as the supporting hand. Place the fingers of the supporting hand horizontally across the dorsal surface of the toes, with the index finger level with the tip of the toes. (**See Figure 9.6**) Place the fingers of the working hand over the outside of the supporting fingers; the first two fingers of the working hand should be over the first two knuckles of the supporting fingers for leverage. **(See Figure 9.7)** Using the basic thumb technique and starting with the great toe, work down the middle and lateral edge of each toe from its tip to its base. The working hand and the holding hand move together as a unit as you move from toe to toe. Remember, the first fingers of the working hand should be over the first two knuckles of the supporting fingers. Be sure to work each toe several times and take about 6 to 10 small bites down the toe.

Then, change hands and repeat this process with the left thumb, starting on the small toe. Always work **down** the middle and then the medial edge of each toe to its base, remembering that the right hand will be supporting and protecting the toes.

This process is repeated on the left foot with alternate hands. Start with the left hand on the left foot.

Several things to remember when working the sinus reflexes:

- These reflexes generally are quite sensitive, especially the 3rd and 4th toes, so relax the pressure a bit when working these reflex areas.

- We generally start to work from the tip of the toe to the base; if the toes are long, you **can** work from the base **upwards**.

- These reflexes are worked for anything in the corresponding zone of the head, including eyes, ears and teeth.

- Helper areas include the ileocecal valve, pituitary and adrenal gland reflexes.

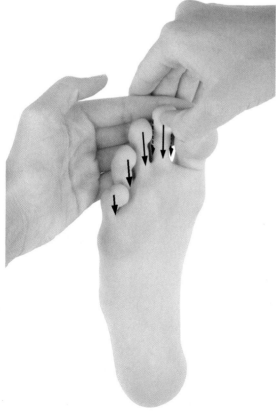

Figure 9.6
Working the sinus reflex

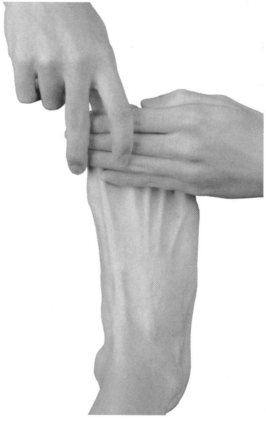

Figure 9.7
Leverage for working the sinus reflex

The Respiratory System is important to the Reflexologist as many respiratory diseases and associative problems are a common occurrence.

Now, let's take a specific look at some particular disorders and corresponding reflex areas to work.

DISORDERS OF THE RESPIRATORY SYSTEM

DISORDER	DESCRIPTION	REFLEX AREAS TO WORK
Adenoids	The so called "pharyngeal tonsils" located in the posterior portion of the nasal cavity. When enlarged, may obstruct breathing.	All toes, pituitary
Asthma	Spasms of the muscles in the bronchial tubes and often an excess secretion of mucus which obstructs the breathing passageways.	Chest/lung, adrenals, ileocecal valve, diaphragm
Bronchitis	Inflammation of one or more bronchi.	Chest/lung, adrenals, ileocecal valve, diaphragm Lymphatic System
Croup	Most often occurring in children, it is a laryngeal spasm which makes breathing very difficult.	Chest/lung, diaphragm, bronchial tubes, ileocecal valve, all toes
Emphysema	A condition where the alveoli and bronchial tubes become over distended by gas or air.	Chest/lung, adrenals, diaphragm, ileocecal valve, kidneys, Lymphatic System
Hay Fever	An allergic disease affecting the mucous membranes of the nose and other respiratory passageways and the conjunctiva of the eyes.	All toes, chest/lung, all glands: esp. adrenals, ileocecal valve, diaphragm
Pleurisy	Inflammation of the pleura, the membrane lining the thoracic cavity and covering the lungs.	Chest/lung, Lymphatic System, adrenals, diaphragm
Pneumonia	Inflammation of the lungs caused primarily by bacteria and viruses.	Chest/lung, diaphragm, all glands; esp. adrenal, ileocecal valve, Lymphatic System
Sinusitis	Inflammation of the sinuses.	All toes, chest/lung, ileocecal valve, adrenals

For a detailed listing of all disorders, see Systems Disorders at the back of this book.

Chapter 10

THE DIGESTIVE SYSTEM

"The fruit thereof shall be for food, and the leaf shall be for medicine."

Ezekiel 47:12

THE DIGESTIVE SYSTEM

While the spine is described as the hollow bony structure containing nerves which run to all parts of the body, the Digestive System is comprised of a tube . . . the alimentary canal, plus a number of accessory organs. (**See Figure 10.1**)

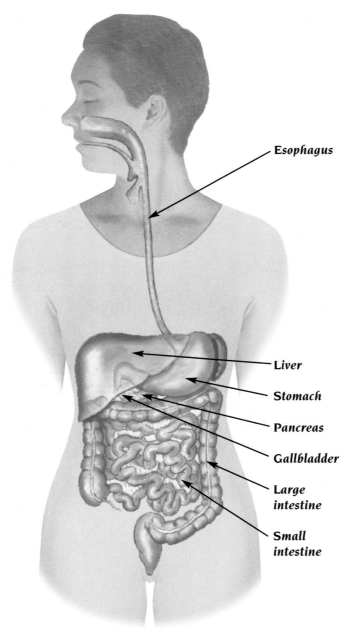

Esophagus

Liver

Stomach

Pancreas

Gallbladder

Large intestine

Small intestine

Figure 10.1
The digestive system

What is meant by digestion? Simply the process by which certain organs act on ingested food both mechanically and chemically so it can be absorbed and thereby provide nutrition for the body.

Digestion is a process that starts in the mouth with the chewing and mixing of food with saliva which contains important enzymes. From this point on, the mixture enters the alimentary canal where food is reduced to soluble, absorbable substances. The usable material is absorbed into the body and the waste material eliminated.

The alimentary canal is formed by the mouth, pharynx, esophagus, stomach, small intestine, colon (or large intestine) and rectum.

The accessory organs associated with the digestive system include the salivary glands, liver, gallbladder and pancreas.

The mouth's primary function in digestion is largely mechanical since the food is broken up by the teeth, ground into small particles and moistened by saliva.

The pharynx serves to pass food from the mouth to the esophagus.

THE ESOPHAGUS

The esophagus conveys food from the pharynx to the stomach – passing through the thorax and then through the esophageal hiatus of the diaphragm to the stomach.

THE STOMACH

In the stomach, vigorous activity takes place to chemically change the food substances into a more absorbable state.

As food enters the stomach, wave-like contractions sweep from top to bottom in order to mix the food with the gastric juices. Located deep within the folds of the stomach's interior are over 35 million glands which secrete up to 3 quarts (2.8 liters) of gastric juices per day. These juices contain hydrochloric acid and pepsin as well as other powerful enzymes needed to break down heavy proteins and other food substances.

The pepsin breaks down the proteins; other juices reduce the food to a semi-liquid consistency called chyme. The amount of time it takes for the stomach to break down food substances varies with the types of food eaten, usually from 3 to 5 hours.

Approximately 85% of the stomach is located on the left side of the body and has a capacity of about 2 quarts (1.89 liters).

The muscular contractions or peristalsis of the stomach churn the food with the enzymes and work it toward the pyloric valve and into the duodenum (beginning of the small intestine).

NOTE: If the stomach acid is not appropriately neutralized in the duodenal area, the acid can irritate the lining which results in an ulcer, a duodenal ulcer. If the ulcer is in the stomach, it is termed a gastric or peptic ulcer.

THE SMALL INTESTINE

The small intestine plays the major part in digestion and absorption of the nutrients from the food. It is divided into 3 sections: the duodenum, the jejunum and the ileum. It is important to note that the bile and pancreatic ducts open into the duodenum. Bile and pancreatic juice are important aids to digestion. They also neutralize the acid from the stomach.

The Ileocecal Valve is located at the end of the ileum at the junction of the cecum which is the first portion of the colon. (**See Figure 10.2**) It is a sphincter valve which controls the passage of the contents from the small intestine.

When the food reaches the large intestine, the digestible parts have already been acted on by enzymes, so basically the functions of the large intestine are absorption of water and mineral salts and the elimination of mucus and waste products.

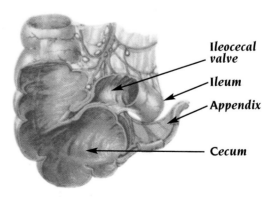

Ileocecal valve

Ileum

Appendix

Cecum

Figure 10.2
The ileocecal valve

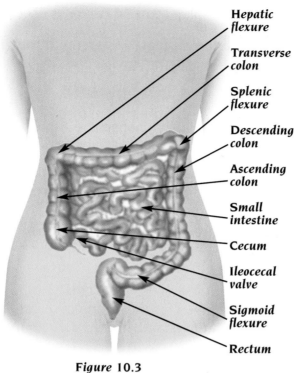

Hepatic
flexure

Transverse
colon

Splenic
flexure

Descending
colon

Ascending
colon

Small
intestine

Cecum

Ileocecal
valve

Sigmoid
flexure

Rectum

Figure 10.3
The large and small intestines

THE LARGE INTESTINE

The large intestine is divided into the cecum, ascending, transverse, descending and sigmoid areas of the colon. (**See Figure 10.3**)

The cecum – is the first portion of the large intestine. The appendix is also located on the blind end of the cecum.

The colon – rises from the cecum as the **ascending** colon on the right side of the body; turns at the hepatic flexure to become the **transverse** colon and then turns downward at the splenic flexure on the left as the **descending** colon. It then makes an "S" turn, forming the portion known as the **sigmoid flexure** part of the sigmoid colon. This is one of the Reflexologist's most difficult reflex areas to work. It then passes into the pelvic region to the level of the sacral vertebrae where it becomes the **rectum.**

ACCESSORY ORGANS TO DIGESTION

The main salivary glands are located just outside the mouth cavity. The saliva produced by these glands consists of approximately 98% water, the balance being made up of inorganic salts and enzymes.

The one important enzyme is ptyalin which begins to digest the starches within the food by breaking them down into more simple forms of carbohydrate sugars.

THE LIVER

The liver is a secreting, spongy type organ weighing about 3 pounds; it has the ability to double its normal size under certain conditions. It is located predominately on the right side of the body in the upper area of the abdominal cavity below the diaphragm and is protected by the rib cage. The liver performs over 500 functions and even takes over some of the functions of the spleen should the occasion arise. It also has the ability to regenerate itself in many cases. But most importantly: if the liver fails, the body dies.

Of chief importance is the liver's metabolic functions, including carbohydrate metabolism. This simply means the formation and storage of glycogen which the liver turns into glucose (a sugar) when it is needed and then releases it into the blood stream. The level of sugar in the blood is delicately balanced by one of the functions of the pancreas . . . the release of the hormones insulin and glucagon. Insulin helps to prevent an abnormally high blood-sugar. If the pancreas does not secrete an adequate amount of insulin, the percentage of sugar in the blood causes the kidneys to react and they excrete excess sugar in the urine. As a result, the glycogen stored in the liver becomes depleted causing serious damage. Glucagon has the opposite function to insulin since it elevates blood-sugar when needed by accelerating the change of glycogen to glucose. (For a fuller discussion on diabetes, **See Chapter 12**, the Endocrine System).

Cholesterol is an essential element of the blood, the precursor of hormones and is controlled in the blood stream by the thyroid gland. It is manufactured within the liver and is also absorbed from certain foods, including animal fats, egg yolk, butter, cream and milk, but it is not found in fruit, vegetables, cereals and nuts.

Today, there is evidence that emotional tension, in addition to its direct effect on the blood vessels, hastens the process of narrowing the coronary blood vessels by interfering with the metabolism of fats and overloading the blood stream with the fatty substance – cholesterol – which thickens the walls of the arteries.

Disturbances within the liver can be indicated by such conditions as continuing fatigue, irritability, sleeplessness and liver pains. To summarize this important organ's contribution to bodily health:

The liver aids in:

- Digestion

- Coagulation

- Metabolism

- Bile formation

- Circulation

- Detoxification

- Blood formation

It destroys poisons and microbes, detoxifies unwanted chemicals, and stores vital vitamins, glycogen, fats, carbohydrates, proteins and minerals, including iron and copper.

Special liver cells (Kupffer) clean intestinal blood before its reentry into the general circulation. Dead body cells are changed into usable items such as bile. Small wonder that the liver reflex lists high in importance.

THE GALLBLADDER

The gallbladder is a muscular, pear-shaped receptacle for bile that is manufactured in the liver. It is attached to the underside of the liver and linked to the duodenum by a duct system. The duodenum is the first looping section of the small intestine.

Bile is secreted by the liver at about 500cc a day. It passes from the liver into the common bile duct, to be stored in the gallbladder. From here it enters the duodenum via the duct.

Bile has, as one of its more important functions, the emulsifying of fats, thus assuring their digestion and absorption. Another function of importance is that it serves as a lubricant in the intestines.

The walls of the gallbladder contain smooth muscles and in its hollow interior is stored some of the bile formed by the liver between meals. The entrance into the intestine of the gastric contents of the stomach (containing hydrochloric acid and fats) not only stimulates bile production by the liver but also causes previously formed bile to be expelled from the gallbladder into the duodenum.

THE PANCREAS

The pancreas functions as both an exocrine gland and endocrine gland. As an exocrine gland, it aids in the digestion process. The digestive juice of the pancreas contains enzymes that break down proteins into amino acids, starch into sugar and fat into a more soluble state. Pancreatic juice is alkaline to combat the acidity from the stomach.

The pancreas is located below the liver and the stomach, and is about 6 inches (152.4 mm) in length and weighs about 3 ounces (85.0 grams). It supplies the fuel to stoke cellular fires for everything from the batting of an eyelid, to the involuntary pumping stroke of the heart.

As an endocrine gland, the pancreas is responsible for the secretion of insulin and glucagon into the blood stream. The release of these hormones is related to the level of glucose (blood-sugar) in the body at any given time. The combined action of insulin and glucagon keeps the blood-sugar at the proper levels and assures that glucose is burned and supplied as needed.

WORKING THE REFLEXES FOR THE DIGESTIVE SYSTEM
(See Figure 10.4)

As previously indicated, digestion starts in the mouth or oral cavity.

Included with the mouth reflex will be the salivary glands which are arranged in pairs: the parotid (in the cheeks in front of the ears), the submandibular (under the jaws) and the sublingual glands (under the tongue). To work these reflexes, look closely at **Figure 10.5**. The mouth reflex is usually found three quarters of the way from the tip of the great toe downward. Slightly above and below this area will be the salivary gland reflexes. The throat reflex is located slightly below this area. To effectively reach this reflex area, work all the way around the toe. The bottom of the toe, of course, is the meaty part; the top of the toe is thinner and, therefore, is a very delicate area. Work all the way around, as well as the sides of the great toe. Work this area using both thumb and finger techniques.

Use the right thumb when working the right foot and vice versa. The basic thumb technique is always used with a forward motion. Support and separate the great toe with the holding hand, and walk across the middle third of the great toe, on the plantar surface of the foot with the thumb. (**See Figure 10.6**) With the same working hand continue with the index finger on the dorsal surface of the great toe from the base of the toenail to the base of the great toe. (**See figure 10.7**) Repeat this several times.

Remember that while working this reflex area on the great toe, you are also working a multitude of other reflexes. This region actually represents the entire throat reflex and, as stated before, this area includes a

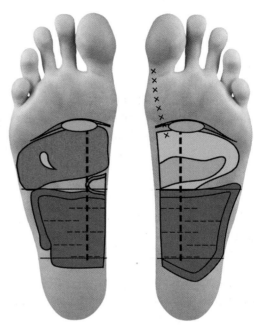

Figure 10.4
Reflexes for the digestive system

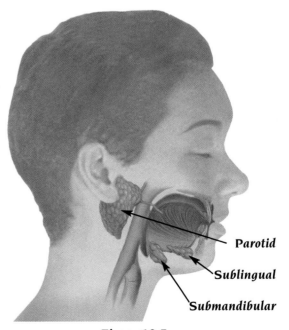

Parotid

Sublingual

Submandibular

Figure 10.5
Salivary glands

115

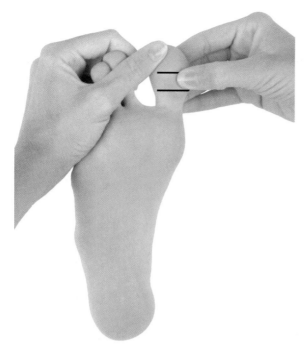

Figure 10.6
Working the salivary glands

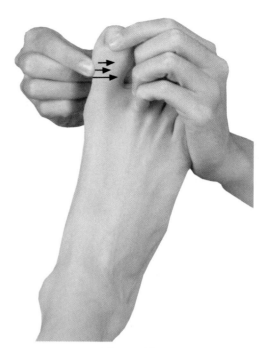

Figure 10.7
Working the salivary glands (dorsal surface)

myriad of reflexes including the salivary glands, the tongue, teeth and the esophagus, as well as the tonsils and the thyroid and parathyroid glands. Remember, the small toes can be used for *fine tuning* this reflex.

Figure 10.8
Esophagus reflex (left foot)

Note that when working this area, it is not an X marks the spot type of working. Also, you must remember just how important it is to work the entire region and not just half of the throat, so work all the way around the great toe of each foot searching for tender reflex points.

ESOPHAGUS REFLEX

Following our food, once it leaves the throat and is swallowed, it is sent down the esophagus to the stomach. Anatomically, our esophagus runs left of the midline. This reflex will be found on the left foot. (**See Figure 10.8**) To work this area, tip the foot out and begin with the left thumb and start at the medial edge of the metatarsal head on the diaphragm guideline and work up to the base of the great toe.   A hiatus hernia is a protrusion of the upper stomach through the diaphragm and will be found at the intersection of the esophageal reflex and the diaphragm guideline. As a helper area, work the entire diaphragm reflex area on both feet for relaxation.

STOMACH REFLEX

The largest part of the stomach reflex is going to be found on the left foot. (**See Figure 10.9**) The stomach reflex, of course, will also extend to the right foot because of its anatomical location within the body. Note that the stomach reflex itself is located below the diaphragm guideline of the foot and above the waistline guideline.

As previously mentioned, a part of the stomach's function is to change the chemistry of the swallowed food. So we should always work the stomach reflex thoroughly. Generally, you will start with the left hand on the left foot and work from the waistline guideline in a criss-cross motion up to the diaphragm guideline and cover the entire region. Use the basic holding technique. Then change hands and come back in the opposite direction, giving the "criss-cross" effect. (**See Figure 10.10**)

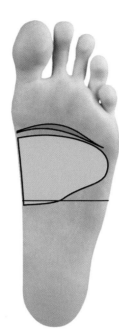

Figure 10.9
Stomach reflex (left foot)

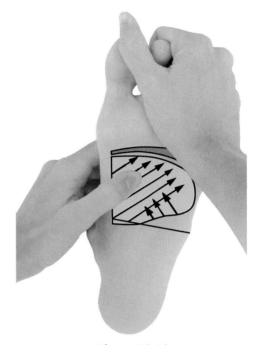

Figure 10.10
Working the stomach reflex

Another important reflex is the duodenal area on the right foot. (**See Figure 10.11**) Start with the right thumb and cover the reflex area approximately at the waistline guideline and is located in the 1st and 2nd zones.

LIVER REFLEX

Sequentially, the next area to work is the liver reflex which is on the right foot, as it is located predominately in the right quadrant of our body. (**See Figure 10.12**) The reflex area covers the space from the waistline guideline to

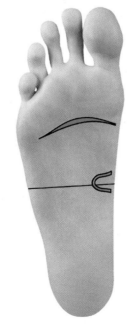

Figure 10.11
Duodenum reflex

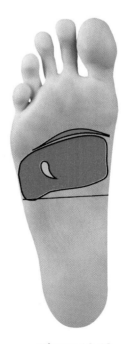

Figure 10.12
Liver/gallbladder reflex

the diaphragm guideline from the medial to the lateral side of the right foot. Being such, the reflex area will be extremely large; when working this area, you have to work it systematically and evenly. Start with the right hand and work the area towards the diaphragm guideline using the basic holding technique. Use those nice and slow creeping motions. Then come back over the area, change hands, and walk across the area in the opposite direction angling towards the diaphragm guideline. (**See Figure 10.13**) It is important, as in any other reflex area, when working the liver reflex for any condition, make sure to work the **entire** area.

Figure 10.13
Working the liver reflex

GALLBLADDER REFLEX

Simultaneously, while working the liver reflex, you are going to be working the gallbladder reflex. The gallbladder is embedded within the liver, so naturally it is much smaller and the reflex area varies sometimes.

Generally, the gallbladder reflex will be around the 3rd or 4th zone above the waistline guideline approximately a third of the way to the diaphragm guideline. (**See Figure 10.12**) This is not an easy reflex to find; sometimes when faced with someone afflicted with gall stones, you must systematically search for the reflex by coming in at different angles.

The gallbladder reflex can also be located on the

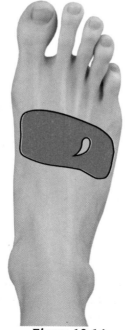

Figure 10.14
Liver/gallbladder reflex (dorsal surface)

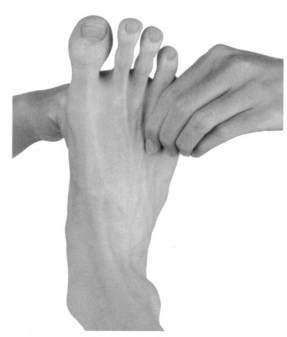

Figure 10.15
Working the gallbladder reflex (dorsal surface)

dorsal surface of the foot just opposite the reflex site on the plantar surface. In other words, after finding the reflex on the plantar surface of the foot, draw a line straight through the foot to the dorsum and work this area. **(See Figure 10.14)**

Many times a person with gallbladder troubles can be worked much more effectively by working the reflex area on the dorsum of the foot. This, of course, will be an extremely sensitive area. If you have a problem locating the gallbladder reflex on the plantar surface of the foot check on the dorsum. For some reason, the dorsum of the foot is easier to work on some people. But be aware that this is a bony area and extremely sensitive and a good reflex technique is necessary. **(See Figure 10.15)**

PANCREAS REFLEX

The pancreas is located in the abdomen, behind the stomach and in front of the spine. **(See Figure 10.16)** It is one of the busiest and most important glands in our body. This reflex area is one which must rank high in importance, so knowing how to work it efficiently and effectively is a must.

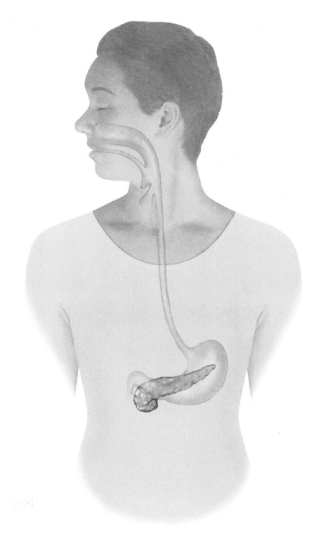

Figure 10.16
The pancreas

The reflex area for the pancreas is found on both feet, but mainly on the left foot and is located slightly above the guideline to the waist to approximately half way to the diaphragm guideline. **(See Figure 10.17)** To work this area, use the basic thumb technique with the left hand, in tiny caterpillar bites, while using the basic holding technique with the right hand. **(See Figure 10.18)** After several slow and complete passes from the medial to the lateral side, change hands and work in the same manner from the other direction. On the right foot the reflex will be slightly below the waistline guideline.

REMEMBER: Just because the pancreas is located deep within the body, it does not mean that you have to dig deep within the foot to locate this reflex. In most cases, this area will be tender, so ease up on the pressure if this is the case. Remember, there are overlapping organ reflexes in this region.

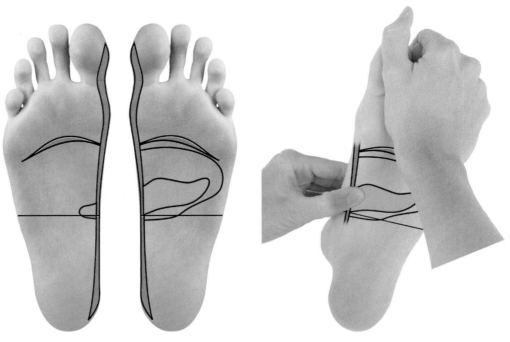

Figure 10.17
Pancreas reflex

Figure 10.18
Working the pancreas reflex (left foot)

INTESTINE REFLEX

Since the intestines occupy such a large area on both sides of the body, you will, of course, work both feet.

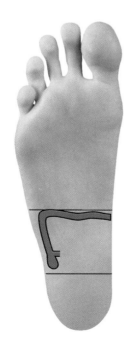

Figure 10.19
Ileocecal valve reflex

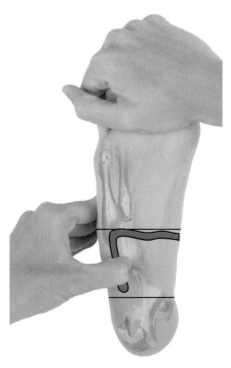

Figure 10.20
Working the ileocecal valve reflex

ILEOCECAL VALVE REFLEX

As you study **Figure 10.19**, note the area where the small intestine empties into the large colon . . . this area is an extremely important one to the Reflexologist since it is the location of the ileocecal valve. This is also an important reflex for the appendix (the appendix is in the area of the ileocecal valve).

NOTE: Tenderness in this area may indicate scar tissue, such as an appendectomy scar . . . it does not always indicate problems.

As you develop your Reflexology skills, you will quickly note that scars and/or adhesions from previous surgery usually will show tenderness in their related anatomical areas. The ileocecal valve reflex is always worked by using the hook-in, back-up technique. **(See Chapter 4)** This reflex area is found on the plantar surface – lateral side (little toe side) of the right foot, below the waistline guideline. To locate this reflex, use the basic holding technique with the right hand and use the left thumb as the working hand. Run the thumb down the lateral edge of the right foot between the waistline guideline and the pelvic guideline into the deepest part of the curve which is about halfway between the two guidelines. Once located, place the thumb in a horizontal position, roll it from the edge of the foot straight around into the reflex. Make sure the thumb is bent at the first joint and use the wrist to hook-in, back-up. This reflex will be fairly close to the lateral edge of the foot on the plantar surface between the 4th and 5th zones. **(See Figure 10.20)**

Once again, the fingers play an important part in giving us leverage by resting them on the dorsum of the foot. This maneuver gives the thumb the leverage it needs to work this difficult reflex area. Place the fingers of the working hand on the dorsum of the foot, drop the wrist while hooking in and backing up.

SMALL AND LARGE INTESTINE REFLEXES

Start on the right foot with the left hand using the basic holding position. Working the area from the waistline guideline to the pelvic guideline for both the large and small intestines. Work across this area first with the right hand and then the left hand with the basic thumb technique using the criss-cross method. Now that this area has been thoroughly worked, proceed to work in a pattern for the large intestine (colon).

Anatomically, as we look at the location of the large intestine, it outlines the small intestine. It comes up from the ileocecal valve reflex toward the waistline guideline on the right foot. This area is referred to *as the ascending colon:*

It should be noted that because the small

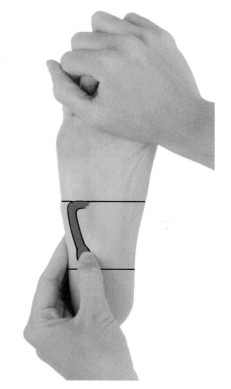

Figure 10.21
Working the ascending colon reflex

intestine and the large intestine are so inextricably positioned that when working the reflex area, you are working both the large and small intestines.

ASCENDING COLON REFLEX

Working the ascending colon on the right foot, use the left hand and walk in a forward motion toward the top of the foot, from the heel towards the waistline guideline, between the 4th and 5th zone. (**See Figure 10.21**) Repeat this process several times working in widening areas.

TRANSVERSE COLON REFLEX

The transverse colon sweeps across the abdominal cavity from right to left, below the stomach. When it reaches the spleen, it bends downward to become the descending colon. To work the transverse colon reflex, work across the waistline guideline on both the right and left foot.

DESCENDING COLON REFLEX

The descending colon extends downwards along the left side of the abdomen to the brim of the pelvis. From this point on, the colon courses in a curve like the letter "S", called the sigmoid colon, or sigmoid flexure.

SIGMOID COLON REFLEX

The way to locate the sigmoid flexure, a pin-point reflex, is to begin on the medial side of the left foot where the heel guideline and the spinal reflex intersect. Note: this area is also called the *bladder reflex*. From this point, angle down at approximate-

Figure 10.22
Sigmoid flexure reflex (left foot)

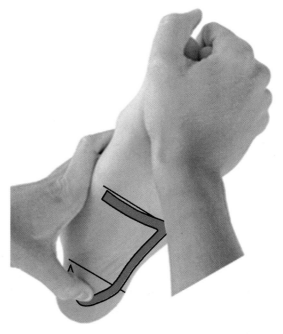

Figure 10.23
Working the sigmoid flexure with the left hand

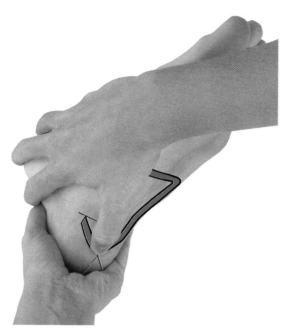

Figure 10.24a
*Working the sigmoid flexure
with the right hand, starting position*

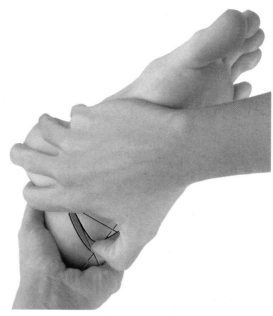

Figure 10.24b
*Working the sigmoid flexure,
hook in, back-up technique*

ly 45° to where the 3-1/2 zone line intersects that angle. (**See Figure 10.22**)

It is imperative that before trying to make contact with this reflex, the heel needs to be worked in several directions with both thumbs to soften up the area.

Use the basic holding technique, tip the foot out with the right hand, the left thumb will walk down the 45° angle from the pelvic guideline to where the lines intersect (3-1/2 zone line) and apply the hook-in, back-up technique at the cross hairs. (**See Figure 10.23**)

After working the whole line downward and using the left thumb for the hook-in, back-up technique, change hands and place the heel of the left foot in the palm of the left hand.

Tip the foot out in a comfortable position and put the fingers of the working (right) hand around the ankle for leverage, making sure the index finger is placed under the anklebone. This prevents contortion of the thumb joint. (**See Figure 10.24a**)

Starting on the medial point of the pelvic line, walk the thumb down at a 45° angle to this pin-point reflex, stop, hook-in, back-up and then repeat the process several times, remembering always to come in at this angle. (**See Figure 10.24b**) It is important to sit back and straighten the arms in order to be the most effective.

The reason for this specific angle is that experience has taught me that this is the **only** effective approach to a most difficult reflex. I have found that many people will ignore working this area because it is callused, thick, difficult to work, and very tiring. This is an important reflex and should be given the same attention as the other reflexes.

Diverticulitis and colitis are some of the problems associated with the colon. The sigmoid flexure reflex is important for problems associated with gas. Often people with chest pains think they are having a heart attack, and find it to be a *gas pocket* initiated in the sigmoid flexure, backing up to the splenic flexure and thus pushing against the diaphragm. This causes pressure against the stomach and heart with subsequent discomfort in the heart area.

I have found that people with varicose veins often have colon problems and working the entire colon reflex may help this condition.

Constipation often starts in the sigmoid region because of a lack of exercise, low fiber diet or other contributing factors. When thinking of colon problems or constipation, it is necessary that you do not just think of working the intestinal tract reflexes. Here is where the helper areas are important. The key helper areas for constipation would be the liver/gallbladder reflex because the liver produces and manufactures the bile, also the diaphragm/solar plexus reflex because emotions have a great effect on our digestive system. Think of working the adrenal gland reflexes, because the adrenal glands help with muscle tone which in turn helps with the peristaltic action in the intestinal tract. Another area to think about is the lower back reflex for the nerves that supply the colon. These are the helper areas that are important to work along with the colon.

DESCENDING COLON REFLEX

Once the sigmoid colon reflex has been worked several times, keep the foot back and

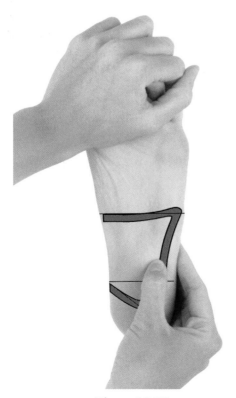

Figure 10.25
Working the descending colon on the left foot

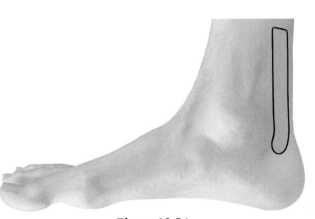

Figure 10.26
The chronic prostate/uterus/rectum and sciatic reflex

straight with the left hand using the basic holding technique and put the right working hand with the fingers beneath the heel. Place the right thumb on the sigmoid flexure reflex and work in a forward motion toward the little toes on the lateral edge up to the waistline guideline . . . this represents the descending colon. (**See Figure 10.25**)

It is important to note here that the primary reason for working **up** the descending colon is because of the leverage advantage using the right hand.

Many people say that you should *massage* the way the material in the colon flows. Let me repeat, Reflexology is not massage . . . it makes no difference what direction you work . . . make several passes up between the regions of the 4th and 5th zones. It should be noted that when working the area from the waistline guideline to the pelvic guideline you are working the intestinal reflexes. Remember to come in at all angles. The two exceptions are the sigmoid flexure reflex and the ileocecal valve reflex . . . the sigmoid reflex is on the left foot and the ileocecal reflex is on the right . . . these two are specific pin-point reflexes which use the hook-in, back-up technique.

RECTUM REFLEX

The sigmoid reflex is very helpful for rectal problems caused by constipation. Constipation causes pressure and can result in hemorrhoids. While softening the heel area in preparation to work the sigmoid flexure reflex, you will be working the rectal reflex. The lower back reflex is also a helper area for rectal problems: the sacral/coccyx reflex area particularly. Often, an injury to this area can affect the rectum. Another area I find helpful is working on the medial side of the leg halfway between the Achilles tendon and the ankle bone in the hollow starting 4 to 6 inches above the anklebone. Gently walk the thumb down the groove on the leg formed between the Achilles tendon and the anklebone. This reflex is called the chronic prostate/uterus/rectum/sciatic reflex. There are many reflexes located in this area. (**See Figure 10.26**) Generally, lack of exercise adds to this problem. For working this reflex, refer to the Reproductive System. (**See Chapter 13**)

To sum up: This chapter is an important one for any practicing Reflexologist: Refer to it often and practice its message repeatedly.

Now, let's take a specific look at some particular disorders and corresponding reflex areas to work.

DISORDERS OF THE DIGESTIVE SYSTEM

DISORDER	DESCRIPTION	REFLEX AREAS TO WORK
Appendicitis	Inflammation of the vermiform appendix.	Ileocecal valve, diaphragm, adrenals, thoracics
Cholesterol	A sterol widely distributed in animal tissues and occurring in the yolk of eggs, various fats and nerve tissues. It can be synthesized in the liver and is a normal constituent of bile. It is the principal constituent of most gall stones.	Thyroid, liver
Cirrhosis	A chronic disease of the liver resulting in the loss of functioning liver cells and increased resistance of flow of blood through the liver.	Liver, all glands: esp. pancreas
Colitis	An inflammation of the colon.	Colon, liver, gallbladder, adrenals, lower spine, diaphragm
Constipation	Difficult defecation.	Colon: esp. sigmoid colon, ileocecal valve, liver, gallbladder, adrenals, diaphragm, lower spine
Diabetes	A disorder of the carbohydrate metabolism characterized by hyperglycemia and glycosuria resulting from inadequate production or utilization of insulin.	Pancreas, adrenals, pituitary, liver
Diarrhea	Frequent passage of watery bowel movements. A frequent symptom of gastrointestinal disturbances.	Ascending colon, transverse colon, liver, adrenals, diaphragm
Diverticulitis	Inflammation of a diverticulum (little distended sacs) in the intestinal tract, especially in the colon which causes stagnation of the feces.	Colon, liver, gallbladder, adrenals, lower spine, diaphragm
Flatulence	Excessive gas in the stomach and intestines.	Sigmoid colon, intestines, stomach, liver, gallbladder, pancreas
Gall Stones	Stones formed in the gallbladder or bile ducts.	Gallbladder, liver, thyroid
Hemorrhoids	A mass of dilated, tortuous veins in the anus and rectum.	Rectum, sigmoid colon, adrenals, liver, lower spine, diaphragm, chronic rectal reflex area

DISORDER	DESCRIPTION	REFLEX AREAS TO WORK
Hernia	The protrusion or projection of an organ or part of an organ through the wall of the cavity which normally contains it.	Intestines, adrenals, Reflex pertaining to location
Hiateal or Hiatus Hernia	Protrusion of the stomach upward into the cavity through the esophageal hiatus of the diaphragm.	Diaphragm, esophagus, stomach, adrenals
Hiccough	Spasmodic periodic closing of the glottis following spasmodic lowering of the diaphragm causing a short, sharp inspiratory cough.	Diaphragm, esophagus, stomach
Hypoglycemia	Deficiency of sugar in the blood.	Pancreas, all glands: esp. pituitary and adrenal, liver
Indigestion	Failure of the digestive function. Symptoms include heartburn, nausea, flatulence and cramps.	Stomach, liver, gallbladder, pancreas, intestines, sigmoid colon, diaphragm
Jaundice	A condition characterized by yellowness of skin due to deposition of bile pigments. It may be caused by obstruction of bile passageways, excess destruction of red blood cells, or disturbances in functioning of liver cells.	Liver, gallbladder, adrenals, thyroid, thoracics
Phlebitis	Inflammation of a vein.	Referral area: arm, adrenals, colon, liver, gallbladder
Tonsillitis	Inflammation of the tonsils.	All toes, Lymphatic System, adrenals, cervicals, neck
Toothache	Self descriptive.	Middle third of great toes, all toes, cervicals, neck
Ulcer	An open sore or lesion of the mucous membrane. A duodenal ulcer is located on the mucosa or lining of the duodenum due to the action of gastric juice. A peptic ulcer is located on the mucosa of the stomach.	Reflex pertaining to location of ulcer: stomach or duodenum, diaphragm, adrenals
Varicose Veins	Enlarged, twisted veins which may occur in almost any part of the body, but usually in the legs.	Referral area: arm, adrenals, colon, liver, gallbladder

For a detailed listing of all disorders, see Systems Disorders in the back of this book.

THE URINARY SYSTEM

". . . They shall lay hands on the sick,
and they shall recover."

Mark 16:18

THE URINARY SYSTEM

The body has a waste collection system which would rival any in the world. A system that works around the clock to get rid of accumulated waste and toxins and to keep the internal environment within the body in a state of equilibrium.

The Urinary System, of course, doesn't do it all. It has help in these functions through the lungs, skin and intestines. They also play an important part in waste excretion.

But it is the Urinary System which is responsible for the elimination of urine that carries most waste products from the cells, waste products which are carried to the kidneys in the blood stream. This intricate system consists of two kidneys, a bladder and two drainage tubes . . . the ureter tubes and the urethra. (**See Figure 11.1**)

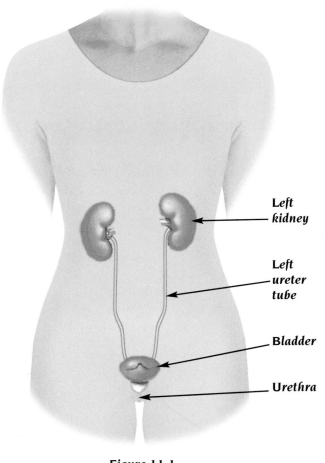

Left kidney

Left ureter tube

Bladder

Urethra

Figure 11.1
The urinary system

The functions of the Urinary System include:

- Maintenance of proper water balance in the body.

- Ridding the body of toxic substances and other waste products, including nitrogen.

- Keeping a proper concentration of salts and other substances in the blood.

- Keeping a balance between acid and base in the body fluids.

It should become increasingly clear that this system is extremely important to the Reflexologist. I constantly stress this to my seminar students and admonish them to always remember that this is the system that eliminates the toxins which are in the blood stream. If we are to maintain a proper balance within the body's systems, we are going to have to become very familiar with the Urinary System and always remember to consider the importance of working these associated reflex areas.

The kidneys are the *master chemists/filters* of the body. It has been estimated that about 1-1/2 quarts (1500cc) of urine are usually excreted by the average adult every day. This filtering system is another of those remarkable aspects of the human body . . . the efficiency of the kidney filtering system can be demonstrated by the fact that it has a filtering capacity of a quart of blood per minute . . . 15 gallons an hour, or 360 gallons (1362.5 liters) a day. It usually filters from the blood about 180 quarts (170 liters) of fluid daily, returning usually 98% to 99% of the water, according to the needs of the body.

The urine which is manufactured by the kidney filters contain, besides water, quantities of urea, uric acid, yellow pigments, amino acids and some minerals. The kidneys are important to remember when discussing gout, kidney stones, edema and high blood pressure.

As the urine is secreted, it leaves the kidneys and enters into the ureter tubes and then into the bladder. From the bladder, the urine is passed to the exterior of the body by the urethra.

Bladder infections are fairly common and are usually more prominent in the female since the female's urethra is shorter than the male's and thus allows infectious organisms easier entry into the bladder. An inflammation of the bladder is called cystitis and is usually caused by bacteria. The kidneys, ureter tubes or bladder may form stones and this leads to painful and difficult urination.

As a Reflexologist, you will often encounter those persons who are suffering from kidney stones. These stones (called renal calculi) are usually composed of calcium oxalate, calcium carbonate, calcium phosphate or uric acid salts. Sometimes a stone made in the kidney will pass into the ureter tube causing intense pain (renal colic).

You can often help these people by careful attention to working the reflexes to the entire Urinary System . . . bladder, ureter tubes and, most importantly, the kidney reflexes.

WORKING THE REFLEXES FOR THE URINARY SYSTEM

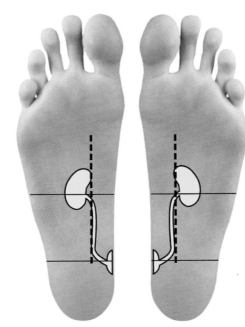

Figure 11.2
Reflexes for the urinary system

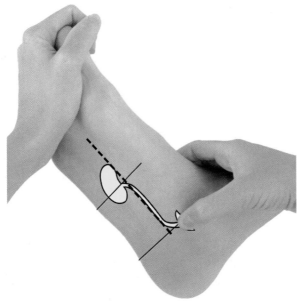

Figure 11.3
Working the bladder reflex

I have noted that many Reflexologists work this system improperly or too hastily; there is a tendency to neglect concentration and needed effort on this reflex area. In my many conversations with seminar students, I find one reason this system does not get its share of attention is that there are so many other organs and systems located within the same region. The students feel that this area has been worked every time the other systems are worked. This may be true when we recall the *packed suitcase* analogy, but it is not true when the person has a definite urinary problem. In this case, a deliberate effort to work the reflexes of the Urinary System will be needed.

I continually stress the fact that a good Reflexologist should always picture the reflexes of the Urinary System as they are projected onto the feet. (**See Figure 11.2**)

The Urinary System reflexes will be located on both feet; the bladder being in the center of the body means that the bladder reflex will be found on the medial edge of both feet, above and below the pelvic guideline.

The kidney reflex is found in the center of the foot above and below the waistline guideline and on the lateral side of the tendon.

The ureter tubes connect the kidneys to the bladder and are located on the medial side of the tendon; between the tendon and the spinal reflex.

To work the Urinary System, hold the right foot using the basic holding technique and with the thumb pushing against the great toe while tipping the foot in a comfortable outward position.

This technique will help to extend the tendon, a very important **guideline** for locating the ureter tubes. (It is important to note that the tendon is only **taut** in order to **locate** the appropriate reflexes and should always be relaxed when working the kidney or any other reflex.)

Use the basic thumb technique on the right foot. Using the right thumb, work through the bladder reflex over to the medial edge of the tendon several times. (**See Figure 11.3**) Then change the direction of your thumb and walk up the ureter tube reflex to the waistline guideline alongside the tendon. Then walk in a forward motion upward and across the kidney reflex which is on the lateral side of the tendon. It is extremely helpful to work the kidney reflex in as

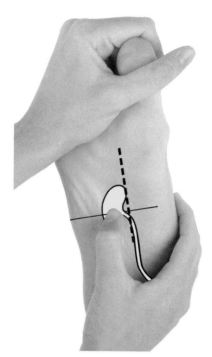

Figure 11.4
Working the kidney reflex

many directions as possible. (**See Figure 11.4**) In the case of kidney stones, I always recommend a high concentration of work on the ureter tube reflexes since this is where the stones usually get lodged. Most pain and consequent problems originate in these tubes.

As for bladder infection, the Reflexologist's trained eye can usually spot chronic bladder problems because in many cases the reflex area will be a bit reddish and *puffy*. Always make sure to work this reflex as any infection of the kidneys can affect the bladder, and vice versa. A bladder infection can easily *back-up* the tubes to the kidneys.

This process of working the Urinary System on the right foot is then reversed when working on the left foot. I recommend that you work with your left hand for the reflex areas of the bladder, ureter tubes and the kidneys; you could also use the right hand to work horizontally across the kidney reflex and down the ureter tube.

HELPER AREAS

The adrenal gland reflexes are helpful in cases of infection. For many of the back problems associated with kidney malfunction, work the nerve reflexes coming off the spinal reflexes. And remember that the parathyroid glands control the calcium balance in the body and so they are a good helper area for kidney stones.

Another affliction, gout, was once called *the rich man's disease* for the simple reason that it was caused by rich foods and wine. It has also been called *metabolic arthritis* by the medical profession and for good reason since it is caused by too much uric acid which in turn results in a build-up of *urates* around the joints. Gout is marked by acute arthritis and an inflammation of one of the joints usually in the knee or foot. With gout, you should always work the kidney reflexes thoroughly.

Another affliction associated with the kidneys is one in which the kidneys themselves become inflamed. It is called either "Bright's disease", or Nephritis. This disease may afflict a portion of the kidney or the entire kidney itself, and may be acute or chronic. In any case, work the entire kidney reflex.

Another important problem associated with this system is called the silent killer . . . hypertension or high blood pressure associated with kidney disease. This disease is marked by a persistent elevation in the blood pressure and is due to a narrowing or blockage in the blood vessels. Some of the results of high blood pressure are cardiac hypertrophy and eventual heart failure; further hardening of the arteries; possible rupture of the blood vessels, especially those in the brain which cause cerebral hemorrhaging or apoplexy. Hypertension can also cause kidney failure or compromise the ability of the kidneys to remove toxic waste from the blood and maintain the fluid, electrolyte and acid-base relationship so necessary for homeostasis. To work the areas associated with high blood pressure, work the diaphragm/solar plexus reflex; as helper areas, work the kidney and endocrine gland reflexes.

As I mentioned, this system is not one which should be just passed over. It is very important to the well being of the entire body and merits your full attention. Go back and study some of the more important aspects of this system; you will be glad you did.

Now, let's take a specific look at some particular disorders and corresponding reflex areas to work.

DISORDERS OF THE URINARY SYSTEM

DISORDER	DESCRIPTION	REFLEX AREAS TO WORK
Anuria	Cessation of the production of urine by the kidneys.	Kidneys, ureter tubes, bladder, adrenals, lower spine
Cystitis	Inflammation of the bladder.	Bladder, kidneys, ureter tubes, adrenals, lower spine
Dysuria	Difficult or painful passage of urine.	Bladder, kidneys, ureter tubes, adrenals, lower spine
Incontinence	Inability to retain urine.	Bladder, kidneys, ureter tubes, adrenals, lower spine
Kidney Stones	Also called renal calculus. Small stones form in the kidney and pass through the ureter usually with intense pain called renal colic.	Kidneys, ureter tubes, bladder, diaphragm, parathyroids, adrenals
Nephritis	(Also called Bright's Disease) an inflammation of the kidney.	Kidneys, ureter tubes, bladder, adrenals, lower spine
Uremia	Toxic condition in which nitrogenous substances accumulate in the blood.	Kidneys, adrenals

For a detailed listing of all disorders, see Systems Disorders at the back of this book.

Chapter 12

THE ENDOCRINE GLANDS

"Behold I will bring it health and healing."

Jeremiah 33:6

THE ENDOCRINE GLANDS
The remote control organs

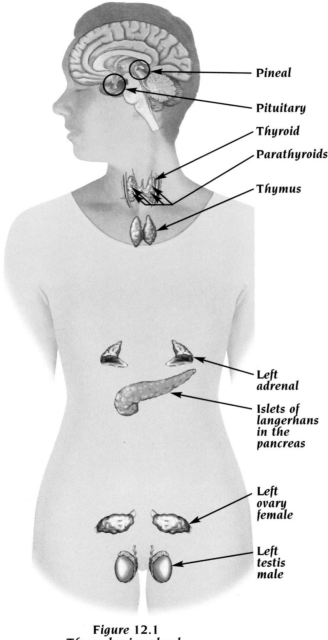

Pineal

Pituitary

Thyroid

Parathyroids

Thymus

Left adrenal

Islets of langerhans in the pancreas

Left ovary female

Left testis male

Figure 12.1
The endocrine glands

Many times during my Reflexology seminars, a sudden quizzical look comes over the faces in the audience when we begin to discuss the Endocrine System. Much has been written in medical literature about these powerful little ductless glands which together constitute the Endocrine System. The *endocrine glands*, along with the Nervous System, are responsible for most of the activities in the body.

I sometimes like to compare them to the thermostat in our homes . . . they are like those remote control devices which keep our houses at just the right temperature. These endocrine glands help the body to adapt to our environment; some of them are even essential to life itself as well as for the smooth operation of all the body's parts.

They are called remote controls for another simple reason: they are ductless and there are no direct "pipe lines" to one special organ. Rather, they produce internal secretions which are discharged into the blood stream or into the Lymphatic System and then circulated to all parts of the body. The internal secretions produced by the endocrine glands are called **hormones** from the Greek I *stimulate*.

Hormones produce profound effects on tissues and organs, many of them remotely located from the site of the origin of the hormone.

I always stress to my Reflexology students the importance of learning the anatomical location of these glands as shown in **Figure 12.1**.

The endocrine glands are sometimes divided into three groups:

- The Pituitary (and the contiguous hypothalamus),

- The Thyroid, adrenal glands (suprarenal) and reproductive glands (ovaries and testes) which are under the control of the Pituitary,

- The parathyroid glands, pancreas, placenta and the gastrointestinal mucosa.

Now, lets take a closer look at these glands and their specific functions.

The 8 main Endocrine Glands which you will be concerned with are:

- The Pituitary, or Master Gland

- The Pineal

- The Thyroid

- The Parathyroid Glands

- The Thymus

- The Adrenal Glands

- The Pancreas

- The Reproductive Glands

THE PITUITARY GLAND

This gland is a rounded body about the size of a pea. It is attached to the hypothalamus at the base of the brain but it has a masterful part to play in the functioning of the body.

The pituitary gland has been termed: the *master gland of the body, general headquarters* of the Endocrine System, and even the *leader of the endocrine orchestra*. It is easy to understand the reasoning behind all of these titles when you realize that this tiny gland is the only one which produces hormones that specifically affect all of the other glands. As a matter of fact, it actually monitors the activities of the other glands.

Its basic hormones control skeletal growth, growth and development of the gonads, maturation of the reproductive cells and secretion of milk by the mammary glands. It also controls the functional activity of the thyroid gland, the islets of the Langerhans in the pancreas, the adrenal cortex and the parathyroid glands. This gland also plays an important function in controlling blood pressure.

I have found the pituitary gland reflex is excellent for reducing fevers and also useful in fainting spells. This gland is also responsible for cellular growth and it should be worked in all cases of extracellular growth whether the growth be benign or malignant.

The pituitary gland is also responsible for body growth . . . how tall or short you are. It should be worked as a normal procedure in all children.

THE PINEAL GLAND

The pineal gland is situated under the brain and is connected to it by a short stalk containing nerves and terminates in the hypothalamus.

The hormone secreted by the pineal gland is melatonin which is influenced by the amount of light entering the eye. The production of melatonin increases at night and diminishes during the day.

The functions of melatonin are to coordinate the circadian rhythms of the body and to inhibit growth and development of the sex organs before puberty.

THE THYROID GLAND

The thyroid gland straddles the windpipe in the mid-portion of the neck. Each of the two lobes of this gland are connected by a narrow isthmus. The functions of this gland are to regulate the metabolism, influence the body's growth, help in the development of the teeth, enhance muscle tone, aid in mental development, and to promote the functional activity of the gonads and the adrenal glands. Practically all of the iodine found in the body is found in this gland and so this reflex is especially important to work since most of that iodine is in the form of an amino acid and is responsible for stimulating the oxidative processes in the tissues of the body. It is also important to work this reflex for weight loss, nervousness, rapid heart beat, overweight problems and dryness of the skin. It is also excellent for the control of the cholesterol level of the blood and for mental sluggishness. This gland has also been called *the third ovary* because of its important affect on those glands in the female.

THE PARATHYROID GLANDS

These little glands, usually four in number, lie within the capsule of the thyroid gland and they are chiefly concerned with the metabolism of calcium and phosphorous and they keep the skeletal system in order. They also affect the nervous and muscular tissues.

They are essential to life itself and sometimes a malfunction of the parathyroid glands causes the calcium and phosphorus of the bones to be carried away in the blood stream with the consequent effect that the bones become light, porous and brittle. This is a helper area for nerves and muscles of the body and also for kidney stones.

THE THYMUS GLAND

The thymus gland is situated behind the upper part of the sternum and consists of two lobes. It is large in children and shrinks in size in adulthood as it is responsible for developing the immune response in children.

The thymus gland promotes the maturation of the T-lymphocyte cells. It belongs to the Endocrine System as well as the Lymphatic System.

THE ADRENAL GLANDS

The adrenal glands are sometimes called *suprarenal glands* as both names indicate location: *above the kidneys*. They are a pair of flattened, yellowish organs about 2 inches high, 1 inch wide and about 1/2 inch thick and are located right above each kidney.

The blood stream is very kind to these two glands since the aorta pumps a rich supply to them, and no wonder when you learn of their importance in body functioning.

Always look at the adrenal glands with their structure as well as their function in mind, since each gland is composed of two organs . . . a convoluted cortex surrounding a medulla.

In embryological development, the adrenal cortex gives origin to the sex glands. The cortex secretes about 50 hormones concerned with bodily strength and sex development. These hormones are divided into 3 groups:

- The body's own internal cortisone-like compounds which regulate sugar metabolism and combat inflammation;

- Electrolyte-regulating hormones that control sodium and potassium and water balance; and

- Sex hormones that supplement those secreted by the gonads.

The medulla secretes the important hormone adrenaline (epinephrine), the activator which works on the Nervous System.

Stressful situations such as worry, anger or fear increase the flow of adrenaline which, in turn, prepares the body for *flight or fight* by initiating:

- An immediate rise in blood pressure;

- Stepped up respiration rate;

- Stimulation of the skeletal muscles thus increasing the capacity for work;

- Increase in the basal metabolism rate and the rate of oxygen consumption;

- Increase in blood sugar by stimulating the liver to release glucose from glycogen.

The adrenal glands are responsible for giving us what I am fond of calling the old *giddy-up-and-go*. When a person is run down and apathetic all the time . . . look to the adrenal glands. Adrenaline also helps to give us the muscle tone we need throughout the body, including that important peristaltic action in the intestines. Adrenaline is also important in the treatment of heart problems as well as asthma.

The importance of adrenaline in checking attacks of asthma can be emphasized by anyone who has had a severe attack . . . the emergency procedure to restore normal breathing is a shot of adrenaline. Relief comes almost immediately.

THE PANCREAS

The pancreas was covered lightly in the Digestive System. (**See Chapter 10**) But, it might be wise to reiterate here, that the pancreas is located behind the stomach. It lies in a horizontal position, the *head* attached to the duodenum, the *tail* reaching to the spleen. The larger portion is found just above the waistline guideline on the left foot and the smaller portion will be partially below the waistline guideline on the right foot.

Remember that the pancreas produces both external and internal secretions. The external secretion, called pancreatic juice, contains alkalinizing bicarbonate and digestive enzymes. The internal secretions are hormones called insulin and glucagon that come from masses of cells called the *islets of Langerhans* scattered throughout the gland.

Insulin and glucagon play a primary role in the regulation of carbohydrate metabolism, including the use of glucose by the tissue cells as well as the formation and conversion of glycogen into glucose in the liver.

THE GONADS OR REPRODUCTIVE GLANDS

The ovaries secrete the female hormones estrogen and progesterone and the testes secrete the male hormone testosterone which are responsible for the control and appearance of the secondary sex characteristics. (These are fully covered in the Reproductive System.)

WORKING THE REFLEXES FOR THE ENDOCRINE GLANDS

PITUITARY GLAND REFLEX

I always recommend examining the great toe when you begin to work the pituitary reflex. Why? Well, Mother Nature has made toes in all shapes and sizes, and since the pituitary reflex represents one of the *target* areas in which we will be using the *pin-point* technique, you must *know the toe*.

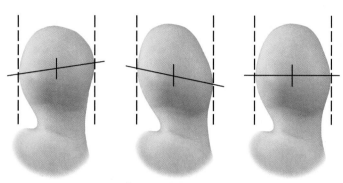

Figure 12.2
Locating the pituitary gland reflex

After years of experimenting, I have developed a special measuring technique which will enable you to pin-point the pituitary reflex. To accomplish this, always look for the widest point on both sides of the great toe and then draw an imaginary line from point to point. Now, there will be many times when you will find that this wide point may be callused, and you will use this callused area for your measurement. Once you have the line drawn, the pituitary reflex will be found at the midpoint of this hypothetical line. As previously stated, the configuration of many great toes will be somewhat different; some lines will run straight across the toe while others may be slightly slanted. This midpoint should be close to the center of the great toe. (**See Figure 12.2**)

Now, to the actual working of this pin-point reflex area – the Pituitary Gland.

It is important when working on the right foot that you use the right hand, and on the left foot you use the left hand. The holding hand will be used to support and protect the great toe. Always cover the toes with the fingers of the holding hand; use the fingers of the working hand for leverage. The leverage fingers are always on the outside of the holding hand. This is done to prevent any injury or unnecessary pain to the top of the great toe.

To work the pituitary gland reflex, always use the medial corner of the thumb of the working hand by utilizing the *hook-in*, *back-up* technique . . . remember the *bumblebee* who sits down and backs up? (**See Figures 12.3a, 12.3b**) Be sure to start this *hook-in*, *back-up* a little beyond the midpoint so that when you pull back you will be directly over the reflex point. Use this technique with a very slight rotation on the pin-point reflex. (**See Technique Chapter 4**) I generally recommend making 3 or 4 working contacts with this reflex area and come back later to repeat this technique.

Figure 12.3a
*Working the pituitary gland reflex
starting position*

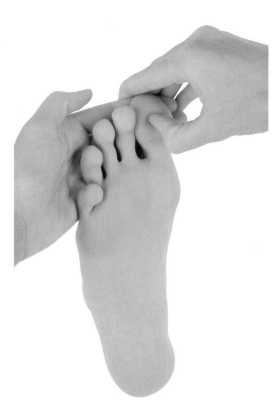

Figure 12.3b
*Working the pituitary gland reflex
hook in, back-up technique*

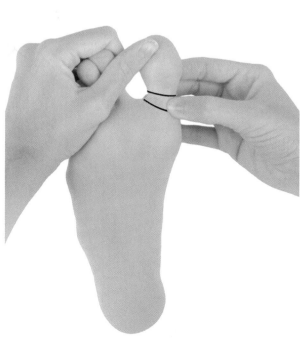

Figure 12.4a
Working the thyroid reflex medial to lateral

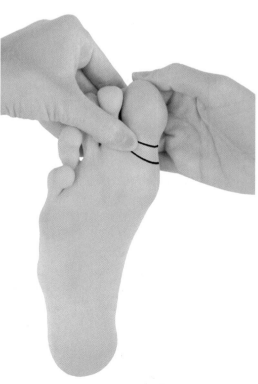

Figure 12.4b
Working the thyroid reflex lateral to medial

THYROID AND PARATHYROID GLAND REFLEXES

Since the thyroid gland is located at the base of the neck area, the reflex area will be located at the base of the great toe.

To work this area effectively, I always recommend holding and protecting the great toe with the holding hand. Use the thumb of the holding hand to spread the great toe so that it may be worked on effectively by the thumb of the working hand. Always place the fingers of the working hand on those of the holding hand.

Using the basic thumb technique, make several passes, walking across the base of the great toe from the medial side to the lateral side. (**See Figure 12.4a**) Change hands, and come back in the opposite direction in the same manner. (**See Figure 12.4b**) This, of course, is done in order to completely cover the comparatively wide reflex area for the thyroid gland reflex. Working several passes in one direction and then changing hands to work in the opposite direction will give you complete coverage of the thyroid reflex area. This will also include the parathyroid gland reflex since they are buried in the thyroid gland.

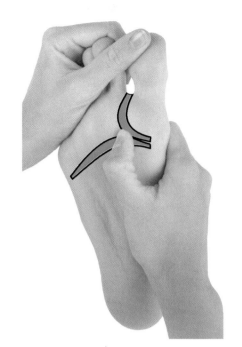

Figure 12.5
Working the reflex relative to the thyroid

HELPER AREA - RELATIVE TO THE THYROID REFLEX

A helper area for the thyroid gland is found between the great toe and the second toe on the plantar surface of the foot. Start where the diaphragm reflex and the spinal reflex intersect and work under the great toe joint and then up the groove between the great toe and 2nd toe. (**See Figure 12.5**) Start with the right hand making several passes. This helps to relax the upper back and throat as well as stimulating the nerves in this area. You could also work the dorsal surface of the foot between the great toe and the 2nd toe.

ADRENAL GLAND REFLEX

The adrenal glands are located on top of

Figure 12.6
Adrenal gland reflex

each kidney. I have already discussed the supreme importance of these glands . . . including the fact that they give us what I am fond of referring to as the *giddy-up-and-go*. Actually, the adrenal glands have over 50 functions to perform.

The reflex areas for the adrenal glands are somewhat complex. Although they lie atop the kidneys, they are in no way related to them. The adrenal gland reflexes are located in the area halfway between the waistline guideline and the diaphragm guideline, on the medial side and next to the protruding tendon. (**See Figure 12.6**)

Work the adrenal gland reflex by holding the foot with the heel of the holding hand on the metatarsal padding and the thumb on the great toe, which, when pushed back, extends the tendon for a landmark.

Use the right hand to work on the right foot and the left hand for working on the left foot. Using the basic thumb technique, walk slowly from the waistline guideline toward the diaphragm guideline. When approximately halfway up this area, you will find a very sensitive area (adrenal gland reflex) on the medial side of the foot right next to the protruding tendon. You can also tip the foot out and with your left thumb work down this same area. This area is often very tender, so be sure to ease up a bit on your pressure when you find this type of situation.

You may also use the pivot rotation technique to work this all important reflex. I have developed this special *pivot* hold for this reflex, which I find works quite effectively. Hold the thumb on the exact reflex area and then flex the foot back and forth on the pivot of the thumb.

Figure 12.7
Working the adrenal gland reflex using pivot point technique

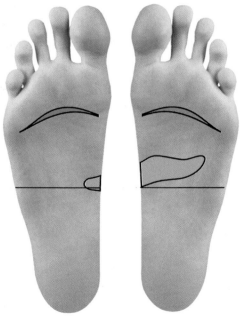

Figure 12.8
Pancreas reflex

(**See Figure 12.7**) (**See Technique Chapter 4**) Be careful not to exert too much pressure initially, rather work up to the desired pressure.

PANCREAS REFLEX

The reflex area for the pancreas is found on both feet but mainly on the left one. (**See Figure 12.8**) On the left foot it is located from the waistline guideline about halfway to the diaphragm guideline. To work this area, use the basic thumb technique in tiny caterpillar bites, while applying the basic holding technique. Continue to work across the entire region several times. (**See Figure 12.9**)

After several slow and complete passes from the initial direction, change hands and work in the same manner from the other direction. On the right foot, the reflex will be partially below the waistline guideline. Work in the same manner as the left foot.

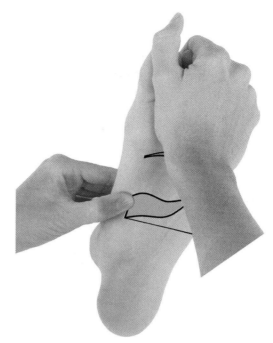

Figure 12.9
Working the pancreas reflex
on the left foot

One of the main concerns you will have when working the pancreas reflex is, of course, diabetes. As a Reflexologist, the first question we ask of a diabetic is, *"How long have you had diabetes?"* There is a rationale in asking this since Reflexology has had its best results with those who have acquired diabetes later in life. This type of diabetes is generally believed to have been initially caused by trauma or shock of some kind. Diabetes is also covered in **Chapter 10**.

The pancreas is one of those organs very susceptible to shock and so, using Reflexology techniques, we have had favorable results with normalizing the pancreas simply by reducing that tension which initially caused the problem.

A person who has suffered from diabetes since childhood may have inherited it, but allergy to self (auto immunity of the pancreas) is known to be involved. This type of condition is more difficult and must be worked on for a much longer time and at short intervals.

A word of caution: Often when working this type of diabetes it is easy to become discouraged since we see no immediate results . . . sometimes it takes months before any results are evident. Generally, the Reflexologist can often help the diabetic with their circulatory and adjunctive problems. Keeping all of the benefits in mind, make sure that you apply a thorough working of both feet; this will help regardless of whether or not the insulin unit dosage comes down. Improving circulation is worth all of our efforts.

Another potential problem in working the diabetic: often they have lost feeling in the foot area. Even when there is no feeling you should work the pancreas reflex as well as all the other helper reflexes.

In the case of the childhood diabetic, you must consider the fact that perhaps the pancreas stopped growing at an early age . . . when the person becomes a little older and more active, the body needs more insulin and the pancreas just cannot keep up with the demand. The Reflexologist cannot help the pancreas to produce the amount needed, but, since the child is still growing, you might be able to assist nature and get the pancreas normalized so that it can continue growth, however small. And, if they are on insulin, less insulin may be required. If the insulin dosage can be reduced, however slightly, you are accomplishing something.

Do not at any time recommend that they alter their medication without first consulting their physician.

Diabetics are sometimes difficult to work with, often for a variety of reasons. Many times they will not stay on their diet if feeling better. Or, when their tests show a slight improvement, they may lower their medication dosage. Always encourage the diabetic to keep in contact with their physician and inform him of any planned change in either diet or medication.

Again, I cannot stress enough the importance of establishing a regular working schedule for the diabetic. I recommend working the diabetic on a regularly established schedule for two, three or even four times a week. Working a short period of time each day would be best even if they were to do their own homework.

And a few words on the opposite of hyperglycemia: hypoglycemia. Hypoglycemia is described as an abnormally low blood glucose level and is usually caused by a rapid and excessive removal of glucose from the blood or from a decreased secretion of glucose into the blood. Overproduction of insulin usually causes this condition. In cases of hypoglycemia (low blood sugar) and hyperglycemia, be sure to work the pancreas, pituitary gland, adrenal gland and the liver reflexes.

The endocrine glands are extremely important in regulating the body's delicate balance. Remember all the glands work together and help one another. Be sure you are familiar with them, their function, and their location.

Chapter 13

THE REPRODUCTIVE SYSTEM

"The fruit of the womb is his reward"

Psalms 127:3

THE REPRODUCTIVE SYSTEM

Life itself is sacred . . . a God given gift to every living thing on this green earth. Consequently, every living thing has a means of reproducing itself in order to perpetuate the species.

With humans, the Reproductive System in the male and the female consists of the primary sex organs and the accessory sex organs. The accessory sex organs have the primary function of uniting the sex cells and then the protection and nourishment of the developing embryo. Also important: the hormones which are produced by these glands and which ultimately influence bodily development and behavior.

Both testes and ovaries serve two functions:

- The production of reproductive cells.

- The production of hormones.

The hormones which stimulate the development of male characteristics are called androgens. The hormone which stimulates the development of female characteristics is called estrogen.

The male Reproductive System consists of the testes, the duct system including the urethra (the duct which leads from the bladder to the outside of the body). The male accessory reproductive glands include the penis, the seminal vesicles and the prostate gland. The prostate is that gland which surrounds the neck of the bladder and the urethra in the male. (**See Figure 13.1**)

The most potent androgenic substance produced by the testes is the principal hormone testosterone which, among other things, affects growth of hair, enlargement of the larynx resulting in a deeper voice, development of height and form and the

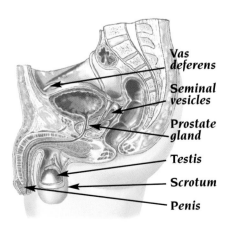

Vas deferens
Seminal vesicles
Prostate gland
Testis
Scrotum
Penis

Figure 13.1
The male reproductive system

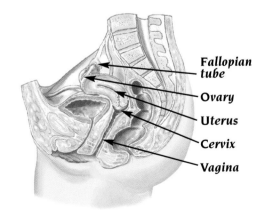

Fallopian tube
Ovary
Uterus
Cervix
Vagina

Figure 13.2
The female reproductive system

150

development of accessory glands, i.e., the prostate and seminal vessels.

In the female, the primary organs of reproduction are the ovaries. The accessory organs are the Fallopian tubes (or oviducts), the uterus and the mammary glands (the breasts). (**See Figure 13.2**)

The ovaries are the source of the estrogen and progesterone which are essential for growth and form as well as for the normal functioning of the genital system. They also regulate cyclic changes in the uterus.

In children, we find these reflexes to be helpful for allergy cases and they should always be worked. They have a lot to do with our well-being and health before puberty and also after the reproductive years of life.

WORKING THE REFLEXES FOR THE REPRODUCTIVE SYSTEM

The uterus or prostate reflex is located on the medial side (great toe side) **approximately** halfway from the high spot on the anklebone to the back corner of the heel at the base of the ridge of the tendon. (**See Figure 13.3**)

To work this reflex on the right foot tip the foot out and support firmly with the holding hand. Place the right hand a few inches above the ankle, with the medial edge of the thumb on the inside of the ankle between the bone and the Achilles tendon. Walk the thumb down this groove. As you walk around the anklebone you will feel a "valley", continue until you reach the high point of the ridge. This is the uterus/prostate reflex. Keep the thumb firmly on the reflex while rotating the foot in an outward direction. Keep the rotations firm by using the natural spring of the ankle joint. This reflex is worked by the rotation of the foot and not by excessive pressure on the reflex point. Repeat several times then repeat on the left foot. (**See Figure 13.4**)

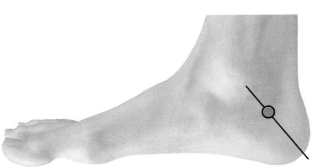

Figure 13.3
Uterus/prostate reflex

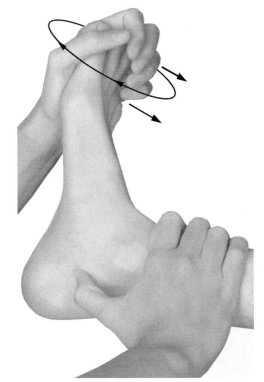

Figure 13.4
Working the uterus/prostate reflex

The ovary and the testicle reflex is found on the lateral side of the heel (little toe side). Find the high spot on the anklebone, square off the back of the heel and draw an imaginary line; divide this line in **half**. This is where the ovary/testicle reflex is found. It is best to use your left index finger on the right foot. Place the finger on this spot where the lines cross and use the slight circular motion. (**See Figure 13.5**) Repeat this on the left foot using the right hand. Helper areas for the ovaries/testes are the thyroid, pituitary and adrenal gland reflexes.

To work the reflex area for the fallopian tubes in the female and the seminal ducts in the male, work the foot where it is joined on to the leg at the ankle (where the foot bends). Remember, the fallopian tubes connect the ovaries to the uterus so visualize this on the foot. The uterus is on the medial side of the ankle, the fallopian tube goes across the ankle from the medial to the lateral side where the ovaries are found. Remember: this area is also for the lymphatic reflex and anything in the groin area.

To work this reflex, hold the foot back and straight. Work with the index finger of the right hand and walk from the medial side starting just under the anklebone to the lateral side finishing just under the anklebone, take at least 20 to 25 bites. Change hands and walk from the lateral side to the medial side of the anklebone. (**See Figure 13.6**) Never pull the foot forward to see what you are doing as this will tighten the area and not allow you to reach this reflex properly.

A nice relaxing technique for this area is called the **ANKLE STRETCH "OVER" TECHNIQUE**. Place the webbing between the thumb and the index finger of the left hand over the ankle of the right foot making sure that all fingers are kept together on the leg. The hand should fit into the groove between the leg and the foot. Exert firm pressure downwards with the webbing between the thumb and index finger. The fingers and thumb should be relaxed and not pressing into the ankle as this causes discomfort to the client. Place the heel of the right hand horizontally on the ball of the foot. The fingers should be on the medial edge of the foot. Push the foot back firmly, then slightly release it, in an oval motion 4 or 5 times in one direction, and then 4 or 5 times in the opposite direction. (**See Figure 13.7**) This will help with swelling of the ankles as well.

A most beneficial helper area for chronic prostate, uterus, rectum and sciatic problems is found in the area of the Achilles tendon. To work this area on the medial side of the right foot, it is best to tip the foot out and push back with your left hand. Wrap the right hand around the lower

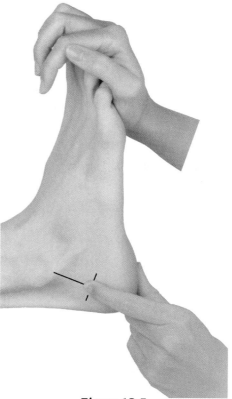

Figure 13.5
Working the ovaries/testes reflex

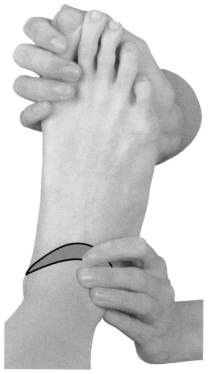

Figure 13.6
Working the fallopian tube reflex

part of the leg, about 6 inches above the ankle, and walk the thumb down toward the heel in the groove between the Achilles tendon and the muscle on the medial side of the leg. (**See Figure 13.8**) This area can be very sensitive so be sure to work it very gently and only to a tolerable threshold. There will be a natural groove formed by the tibia bone in this area, so work this area all the way down to the uterus/prostate reflex. I find that working down is better than working up because we often have a tendency of pinching with our fingers on the lateral side of the leg.

This reflex area is excellent for prostate problems, menopause, menstrual problems, hemorrhoids, and sciatica.

The mammary glands (breasts) are also part of the Reproductive System. When you are working this reflex area, you are also working the chest/lung area. The breast reflex is best worked on the dorsum of the foot from the base of the toes to the diaphragm guideline. The working of this area is found under the Respiratory System (**Chapter 9**). This reflex area is helpful for lumps and soreness in the breasts. Helper areas include the pituitary reflex and the entire Lymphatic System reflexes.

A WORD ABOUT PREGNANCY

Reflexology has been found to be quite helpful during the entire gestation period. In my opinion, and from my experience over the years, Reflexology may help for some of the associative problems of pregnancy including edema and morning sickness. It is also very helpful in relaxing the entire body during the actual delivery period. I have found it is beneficial to work on the person on a regularly scheduled basis during pregnancy. Prenatal care is so important.

While on the subject of pregnancy, I have found that Reflexology has proved to be

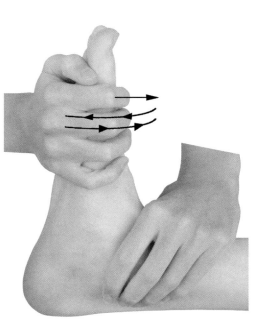

Figure 13.7
Ankle stretch relaxation "over" technique

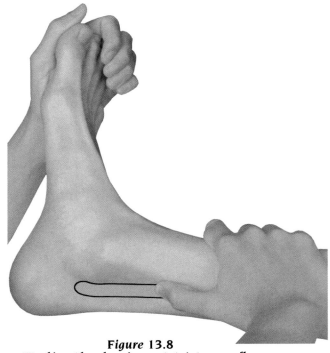

Figure 13.8
Working the chronic prostate/uterus reflex

very beneficial as an aid in fertility. Several scientific recordings show that the sperm count has increased as a result of Reflexology.

Of course, this subject leads us to another about which I have received many questions during the seminars . . . the question of hysterectomies.

Hysterectomy is the removal of the uterus and is often accompanied by removal of the ovaries. There is often some surgical *shock* to the basal system. If a person is scheduled for this type of surgery, it is very advantageous to work **before** the scheduled surgery and also immediately after. An important thing to remember is that the estrogen supply is diminished when the ovaries are removed. The adrenal glands must compensate for this. It is important to work the adrenal gland reflexes as well as the thyroid and the pituitary gland reflexes in order to stimulate the needed hormones. The adrenal gland reflexes are ideal helper areas as are the thyroid and the pituitary gland reflexes. You will also note that all endocrine gland reflexes are usually very sensitive in a person who has had a hysterectomy.

Now, let's take a specific look at some particular disorders and corresponding reflex areas to work.

DISORDERS OF THE REPRODUCTIVE SYSTEM

DISORDER	DESCRIPTION	REFLEX AREAS TO WORK
Hysterectomy	The removal of the uterus and sometimes the ovaries and fallopian tubes.	Uterus, ovaries, fallopian tubes, pituitary, adrenals, thyroid, chronic uterus area, diaphragm
Impotence	Lack of power: chiefly of copulative power of virility.	Testes, prostate, all glands, lower spine, diaphragm
Infertility	Diminished or absent capacity to produce offspring.	Reproductive System, all glands, lower spine, diaphragm
Lump in Breast	Swelling of the lymphatic tissue in the breast.	Chest/lung, Lymphatic System, pituitary
Menopause	When the body flushes during the change (hot flashes) of life.	Reproductive System, all glands: esp. pituitary, adrenal and thyroid, chronic uterus area, diaphragm
Menstrual Cramps	Self descriptive	Uterus, ovaries, fallopian tubes, all glands: esp. pituitary, thyroid and adrenals, lower spine, diaphragm
Morning sickness	Feeling of nausea during pregnancy.	All glands, diaphragm, stomach
Ovaries (cysts)	A foreign growth in the ovary.	Ovaries, uterus, fallopian tubes, all glands: esp. pituitary
Pre-natal care	Healthful care during pregnancy.	Reproductive System, all glands, whole spine, bladder, diaphragm
Prostate problems	Inflammation/enlargement of the prostate gland.	Prostate, all glands, bladder, lower spine, chronic prostate area

For a detailed listing of all disorders, see Systems Disorders at the back of this book.

Chapter 14.

SUGGESTED PROCEDURE FOR A REFLEXOLOGY SESSION

"And that ye study to be quiet, and to do your own business, and to work with your own hands, as we command you;"

1 Thessalonians 4:11

SUGGESTED PROCEDURE FOR A REFLEXOLOGY SESSION

We have developed this book by discussing the various systems of the human body and the reflexes associated with those systems. This is done only to acquaint you with the human body and unless you are a physician this **should not** be discussed with your clients during a session. **We are not physicians nor do we take the place of a physician!** Because of the importance of this fact, let me add a few other admonitions:

We do not combine our work with the selling of other items . . . this could be construed as prescribing and we **never, in any instance, prescribe anything!**

Nor do we treat for specific conditions. Reflexology helps the body to establish homeostasis . . . to seek a natural balance between the systems. I would caution you to reread the above and to always let it serve as your professional guideline.

REMEMBER: If your client has a specific medical problem and has not seen his physician, you should recommend that he do so.

Before beginning, make sure your nails are short and if your hands or your client's feet are perspiring, you may use corn starch.

Now, let me suggest that you use a systematic treatment program during your training, as this helps you to be thorough and not leave parts of the session out. The following session procedure is an example of such a program. Let me also say that once you are a professional Reflexologist your treatment strategy will be based on the present condition of your client, using the helper areas for the specific conditions as the cornerstone of the treatment program.

If your client is new, remember to "meet the feet". Always check for corns, calluses, ingrown toenails, or any other area which might cause discomfort through direct contact.

I always find it best to begin all sessions by initially using all the relaxing techniques on the feet to relax the client and to get their feet accustomed to my hands. (**See Technique Chapter 4**) I also work the diaphragm/solar plexus reflex to further relax the client.

DIAPHRAGM REFLEX TO THE BASE OF THE TOES

Begin working with the right hand on the plantar surface of the right foot in the metatarsal area: the chest/lung reflex area.

After working this area thoroughly with both hands, work this same chest/lung area on the dorsum of the foot with the index finger. Remember to work both the dorsum and the plantar surface from the base of the toes to the diaphragm guideline and from the medial side of the foot to the lateral side. Be sure to work the shoulder reflex all around the little toe joint while working in this area. Another important area in this section, is between the great toe and the second toe.

EYE AND EAR REFLEXES

Next, work the eye and ear reflexes at the base of the small toes by "walking the ridge" with the lateral or outside edge of the thumb. "Walk the ridge" several times in both directions. It is usually most sensitive between the 2nd and 3rd toes.

As you are working be sure to use the relaxation techniques often to keep the client more relaxed. If you don't, they will tense up.

ALL THE TOES

Now that the client is accustomed to your hands, proceed up to the toe reflexes. Starting with the great toe, work the reflexes to the cervical spine, thyroid gland, side of the neck, brain and pituitary gland making sure to work the entire great toe very carefully and systematically. It is also very beneficial to work the dorsal side of the great toe, especially for thyroid problems. Then on to the small toes covering the center and both sides from the tip to the base.

The toes may be very sensitive so remember to start lightly and gradually increase the pressure.

DIAPHRAGM GUIDELINE TO PELVIC GUIDELINE

The next area to be worked is the soft tissue area of the foot between the diaphragm guideline and the heel. This area contains most of the reflexes to the major organs so remember to work this area systematically from all angles. It is a must to have smooth, even pressure or you will miss some important areas. Do not forget the special techniques for the ileocecal valve reflex on the right foot.

HEEL AREA

Now you are down to the heel area where it is tough and callused. You will need good leverage and technique to work this area. This area is for the reflexes to the lower back, recum, heel spurs and also the sciatic nerve which passes under the heel. The sigmoid flexure reflex (found on the left foot) is very important, so remember the 45° angle and the hook-in, back-up technique.

SPINAL REFLEX

When you are working across the plantar surface of the foot you will have touched on the spinal reflex and also the lateral muscles of the spine.

As the spine is so important to the whole body, work the entire spinal reflex from the base of the heel to the base of the nail of the great toe. Change hands and work down the spinal reflex. If there is tenderness in a specific area work across this area to be sure you have covered it thoroughly.

ANKLE AREA

Work around the ankle for the reproductive system reflexes; the uterus/prostate on the medial side, the ovaries/testes on the lateral side and fallopian tubes which run across the ankle (this area is also the reflex for the groin and Lymphatic System). While we are on the lateral side of the anklebone, work the pelvic area which includes the hip/sciatic reflex under the ankle bone and the knee/leg reflex in front of the anklebone.

Last, but not least, is the chronic rectum/prostate/uterus/sciatic reflex on the medial side of the leg. Be sure to work down the groove on the medial side of the leg to the uterus/prostate reflex (it is usually better working down the leg than up the leg).

A good Reflexologist will maintain contact with the foot at all times throughout this whole process.

After thoroughly working the one foot, change to the other foot and work in the same sequence as described above.

When completed, return to the original foot and concentrate on any tender areas you may have found. Return to the second foot and work those tender areas again.

I always recommend ending the session with relaxing techniques since this leaves the client with a wonderful relaxed feeling. My favorite one to finish a session with is the metatarsal kneading and then the diaphragm deep breathing technique.

SOME HELPFUL HINTS

I have found that it is very beneficial when working a full session to always use a relaxing technique between each section of reflexes. For instance, after working the toes, I always use the side-to-side relaxation technique. You will find that this is very helpful, particularly on a sensitive foot. The more sensitive a person is, the more the relaxing techniques should be used. Just remember to use that relaxer which is appropriate to the region you are working. If you will go back and glance at the relaxing techniques that have been discussed in **Chapter 4**, you will find that the choice for each reflex area is an easy one.

I am often asked why I work one whole foot and then change and work the entire other foot. I have found that when the entire foot is worked systematically, it actually feels better and allows you to really become acquainted with the anatomy of the foot upon which you are working. There is also a better pattern of performance and you will not miss any areas this way. To make it clear: you are actually "programming" your technique into a standard pattern that systematically covers every area of the foot.

Experience has shown that the client benefits more when it is done this way and it feels much better than constantly switching from one foot to the other.

THE LENGTH OF TIME FOR EACH SESSION?

The average session is usually 30 to 40 minutes and can, of course, vary with your experience as an operator. An initial session with a new client could take up to an hour since you will need to indoctrinate the person with the basics of Reflexology. It is imperative that you explain that you do not diagnose, prescribe or treat for a specific condition. I highly recommend a pre-printed form explaining all of this which should be signed by the client before beginning the first session.

HOW MUCH PRESSURE DO YOU USE?

Naturally, the pressure used will vary with each pair of feet. The more sensitive the individual, the lighter the pressure. One sure way to check the right pressure is to watch the client's face to see if you are causing any discomfort. A note to the beginner: you will develop a "sense of touch" as you work and you will soon learn that some discomfort may be experienced by the client. The trained Reflexologist soon learns to distinguish between real discomfort and a "good hurt". Divergent as that statement may seem, you will learn that one of the high points in a session is when you reach that level where your client tells you that "it hurts, but it feels so good".

HOW MUCH TIME IS SPENT ON EACH FOOT?

The best way to approach this is to divide your time into sections . . . ten minutes per segment. That's ten minutes per foot and then the last 20 minutes should be devoted to those reflexes which need more attention. This will vary with the client's condition.

HOW MANY SESSIONS PER WEEK?

For optimum results, I recommend a minimum of two sessions per week for several weeks and then gradually reduce the number per week. Of course, the more chronic the problem, the more often and the longer Reflexology must be used.

Always remember, one does not have to be sick to enjoy the benefits of Reflexology. It is used as a "toner upper" by many people. To others, it is employed as a preventive, or a holistic approach to health. In these cases, I recommend a session once a month, or even once every two weeks. This will depend on what it takes to maintain homeostasis for the individual.

WHAT FOOT SHOULD YOU START ON?

As my aunt Eunice found out so many years ago, it really doesn't make any difference. I have always started on the right foot using the right hand. My recommendation is to start with that foot with which you are most comfortable. After a while, it will become almost automatic with you.

It should be noted that these holding and working positions may vary slightly for several reasons . . . the size of the foot or the practitioner's hands . . . this is particularly true when working with children's feet.

Let me finish this section by perhaps repeating myself. But it is important for you to always remember that Reflexology is an adjunctive to the health field, the same as the other modalities. **We do not practice medicine**. Often when in a session and you come upon a tender spot, your client might ask you what that represents or what does that spot mean health wise. Your **best** answer to that is that it simply represents a region of the body. Example of a region: a.) Head region, b.) Chest region, c.) Mid-section, d.) Pelvic region. You cannot tell them that it represents a specific organ or gland. Since so many organs and glands overlap, you might be wrong in your answer anyway. You are helping nature to normalize. Tenderness indicates congestion and we are simply trying to work that out with a series of sessions, but we must always realize that there are exceptions to this . . . some people are more sensitive, some are ticklish. And the opposite is often true. They may have no tender spots and still have ill health. Often, certain medications tend to anesthetize reflexes, poor circulation and a high pain threshold may often negate reflexes. On a heavy foot, the reflexes are sometimes deeper and will require more precise heavy pressure. Sometimes it will take two or three sessions to bring about the sensitivity. When a person is very ill, you should work for a short period of time, very lightly and more often.

REMEMBER: If you overwork the client he/she may have a reaction. A reaction might be uncomfortable but is not harmful as it is nature's way of carrying away toxins. This reaction usually does not last long and can be considered as a "healing crisis".

There are many ramifications to this science of Reflexology. If you follow the rules and the training, making sure you are always aware that "you are not taking the place of the physician", you will succeed. Reflexology is an adjunct to the health field.

Chapter 15

INTRODUCTION TO HAND REFLEXOLOGY

*"So they strengthened their hands for this
good work"*

Nehemiah 2:18

INTRODUCTION TO HAND REFLEXOLOGY

There seems to be an increasing interest today in Hand Reflexology. This is an interesting evolution of interest but one with some ramifications. In my many years of experience with my aunt, Eunice Ingham, and with the experience of colleagues, we have found that there are basic differences between the feet and hands.

- the hands are exposed all the time so they are less sensitive than the feet

- anatomically they are different

- the reflexes on the hands are more compressed than on the feet

- the working techniques are different

Hand Reflexology has proved to be a very effective form of therapy in conjunction with Foot Reflexology. When the hands are treated first the client is very relaxed, paving the way for increased benefits from the Foot Reflexology session.

Hand Reflexology may be used on its own as well as for "homework". This is especially useful when a client is unable to receive treatment as often as is necessary for lasting results. Hands are easy, very accessible and can be worked on anywhere and anytime.

Just think how many times you have waited in a long line, sat in a doctor's office or you were just sitting and watching television! This time can be turned into a profit; a profit for your own health. It is also very helpful as a first aid measure – for that toothache, headache, stress, backache and other ailments.

In the case of an injured foot or if a foot is missing, then working the hands becomes a necessity.

There is another occasion which must be mentioned. There are times when you will meet a person who is either very sensitive or a bit shy about you working on their feet. In special cases like these, working the hands will solve this problem.

For information on my latest book, "Better Health with Hand Reflexology", that teaches the benefits and techniques of Hand Reflexology contact :

Ingham Publishing, Inc.
PO Box 12642
St Petersburg, FL 33733-2642
(727) 343-4811
Website: www.reflexology-usa.net

Chapter
16

INTERNATIONAL INSTITUTE
OF REFLEXOLOGY ®

*"There must be perfect harmony among the
various parts of the body"*

Galen (2nd Century Physician)

INTERNATIONAL INSTITUTE OF REFLEXOLOGY®

The *International Institute of Reflexology* was formed in 1973 to carry on the great work of Eunice Ingham and spread the word about *The Ingham Method® of Reflexology* throughout the world.

The *International Institute of Reflexology* is headed by Dwight C. Byers, today's leading authority on Foot and Hand Reflexology. Mr. Byers is the nephew of the late Eunice Ingham, the originator who researched and developed Reflexology as it is known today throughout the world.

The *International Institute of Reflexology* is the **only** authorized organization that teaches *The Ingham Method of Reflexology*. Their experienced and knowledgeable staff provide the **best** training experience possible on an INTERNATIONAL basis.

We present a concentrated, dynamic presentation on the theory and techniques. After you read this technical book you will want to attend one of our seminars and learn these techniques properly, as you cannot learn this from books alone. The seminars consist of lectures with many visual aids and you will personally apply and receive these techniques. Once you take your first seminar you become a lifetime member of the *International Institute of Reflexology*, which entitles you to attend future **I.I.R.** sponsored seminars, anywhere and as often as you desire at a member rate.

The *International Institute of Reflexology* offers its members several levels of training. Remember the importance of continuing education which enables the practitioner to keep up with the latest developments in the field, while fine tuning their skills and knowledge. The **I.I.R.** maintains a **WORLD-WIDE** referral service, therefore it is important to keep current with the Ingham Method of Reflexology® in order to remain an active Reflexologist for this referral service.

These seminars are for everyone . . . professional and lay people alike.

If you wish to receive information regarding seminars offered in your area or related books and charts, write to:

International Institute of Reflexology ®
PO Box 12642
St. Petersburg, Florida 33733-2642 U.S.A.
Phone: (727) 343-4811 Fax: (727) 381-2807

website: www.reflexology-usa.net

SYSTEMS DISORDERS

The following pages represent a compilation of those disorders with which the practicing Reflexologist should become familiar.

The disorders and their associative reflexes are listed *only* as a guide to help you become more proficient in working these areas.

In no way is this list to be construed as, nor used for, diagnostic purposes. Diagnosis is the prerogative of the physician. *Reflexologists do not diagnose nor prescribe at any time in any manner.* D.C.B.

DISORDER	REFLEX
Acne	All glands: esp. thyroid and adrenal, liver, kidneys, intestines, diaphragm
Adenoids	All toes, pituitary
Alcoholism	Liver, pancreas, diaphragm
Anemia	Spleen, liver
Angina Pectoris	Chest/lung/heart, cervicals, thoracics, adrenals, diaphragm, sigmoid colon
Ankles (swollen)	Adrenals, kidneys, Lymphatic System, referral area:wrist
Anuria	Kidneys, ureter tubes, bladder, adrenals, lower spine
Appendicitis	Ileocecal valve, diaphragm, adrenals, lumbar
Arms (Hands)	Cervicals, upper thoracics, neck, shoulder, referral area: leg, foot
Arteriosclerosis	All glands: esp. pancreas and thyroid, liver, work entire foot
Arthritis	Reflex to affected area, kidneys, all glands, diaphragm, entire foot
Asthma	Chest/lung, adrenals, ileocecal valve, diaphragm
Atherosclerosis	All glands: esp. pancreas and thyroid, liver, work entire foot
Bed Wetting	Bladder, kidneys, ureter tubes, adrenals, diaphragm, lower spine

DISORDER	REFLEX
Bell's Palsy	All toes, cervicals, neck, diaphragm, parathyroids
Bladder Problems	Bladder, kidneys, ureter tubes, adrenals, lower spine
Breasts (lumps)	Chest/lung/breast, lymphatic system, pituitary
Bright's Disease	Kidneys, ureter tubes, bladder, adrenals, lower spine
Bronchitis	Chest/lung, adrenals, ileocecal valve, diaphragm, Lymphatic System
Bunion	Work around and directly on the bunion
Bursitis	Reflex to affected area, adrenals, parathyroids, referral area to affected area
Calluses, Corns	Around and directly on corns or calluses
Carpal Tunnel Syndrome	Cervicals, upper thoracics, neck, shoulder, referral area: ankle
Cataracts	Eye reflex, all toes, neck, cervicals, kidneys, pituitary
Chest Pains	Chest/lung/heart, adrenals, cervicals, thoracics, diaphragm, sigmoid colon
Childhood Diseases	All glands: esp. thymus, spleen, diaphragm, whole spine
Cholesterol Level (high)	Thyroid, liver
Chronic Fatigue Syndrome	Spleen, all glands: esp. pituitary, whole spine, Lymphatic System, all toes
Cirrhosis is of the Liver	Liver, all glands: esp. pancreas
Coccyx (lower backache)	Lower spine, pelvic area, hip, shoulder, cervicals
Colds	All toes, chest/lung, pituitary, adrenals, ileocecal valve, Lymphatic System
Colitis	Colon, liver, gallbladder, adrenals, lower spine, diaphragm
Conjunctivitis	Eye reflex, all toes, cervicals, neck, adrenals
Constipation	Colon: esp. sigmoid colon, ileocecal valve, liver, gallbladder, adrenals, diaphragm, lower spine
Coronary Occlusion	Chest/lung/heart, cervicals, thoracics, adrenals, diaphragm sigmoid colon
Cramps (feet, legs, etc.)	Parathyroids, adrenals, lower spine, pelvic area, hip/sciatic, knee/leg

DISORDER	REFLEX
Cramps (menstrual)	Uterus, ovaries, fallopian tubes, all glands, lower spine, diaphragm, chronic uterus area
Crohn's disease	Small intestine, adrenals, ileocecal valve, liver, spleen, thoracics, diaphragm
Croup	Chest/lung, diaphragm, bronchial tubes, ileocecal valve, all toes
Cystitis	Bladder, kidneys, ureter tubes, adrenals, lower spine
Deafness	Ear reflex, cervicals, neck, all toes
Diabetes	Pancreas, adrenals, pituitary, liver
Diarrhea	Ascending and transverse colon, liver, adrenals, diaphragm
Diverticulitis	Colon, liver, gallbladder, adrenals, lower spine, diaphragm
Dizziness	Ear reflex, cervicals, neck, all toes
Drug Addiction	All glands, diaphragm, liver, kidneys
Dry Skin	Thyroid, adrenals
Dysuria	Bladder, kidneys, ureters, adrenals, lower spine
Ear Infection	Ear reflex, all toes, cervicals, throat/neck, adrenals, (eustachian tube)
Eczema	All glands: esp. adrenal and thyroid, liver, kidneys, intestines, diaphragm
Edema	Adrenals, pituitary, Lymphatic System, kidneys
Emphysema	Chest/lung, adrenals, diaphragm, ileocecal valve, kidneys, Lymphatic System
Encephalitis	All toes, all glands: esp. adrenal
Epilepsy	All toes, cervicals, neck, all glands, diaphragm
Eye Conditions	Eye reflex, all toes, cervicals, neck, kidneys
Fainting	Pituitary
Fatigue (general)	All glands: esp. thyroid, adrenals and pituitary, whole spine, diaphragm
Feet (cold and sweaty)	All glands: esp. thyroid, liver, intestines, kidney, lower spine
Fever	Pituitary

DISORDER	REFLEX
Flatulence	Sigmoid colon, intestines, stomach, liver, gallbladder, pancreas
Fluid Retention (edema)	Adrenals, pituitary, Lymphatic System, kidneys
Fracture	Reflex to affected area on foot, also referral area, parathyroids, diaphragm
Gall Stones	Gallbladder, liver, thyroid
Gas Pains	Sigmoid colon, stomach, diaphragm, intestines, liver, pancreas
Glaucoma	Eye reflex, cervicals, neck, all toes, kidneys
Gout	Reflex to affected area, kidneys, all glands
Grave's Disease	All glands: esp. thyroid, pituitary and adrenal
Growths (abnormal)	Pituitary, reflex to affected area
Hay Fever	All toes, chest/lung, all glands: esp. adrenal, ileocecal valve, diaphragm
Halitosis	Stomach, liver, intestines, all toes
Headache (general)	All toes, whole spine: esp. cervicals, lower spine, diaphragm, all glands
Heart Attack	Chest/lung/heart, adrenals, cervicals, thoracics, diaphragm, sigmoid colon
Heartburn	Esophagus, stomach, gallbladder, all glands: esp. pancreas, diaphragm
Heart Conditions	Chest/lung/heart, diaphragm, cervical and thoracic spine, adrenals, parathyroids, sigmoid colon
Hemorrhoids	Rectum, sigmoid colon, adrenals, liver, lower spine, diaphragm, chronic rectal reflex
Hernia (inguinal)	Groin area, intestines, adrenals
Hiatus Hernia	Diaphragm, esophagus, stomach, adrenals
Hiccoughs	Diaphragm, esophagus, stomach
High Blood Pressure (hypertension)	Diaphragm, kidneys, pituitary, adrenals, thyroid
Hip Pain	Hip/sciatic, pelvic area, lower spine, knee/leg, shoulder
Hot Flashes	Reproductive System, all glands: esp. pituitary, adrenal and thyroid, chronic uterus area, diaphragm

DISORDER	REFLEX
Hyperactivity	Diaphragm, all glands: esp. adrenal
Hypoglycemia	Pancreas, all glands: esp. pituitary and adrenal, liver
Hypotension	Adrenals, pituitary, thyroid
Hysterectomy	Uterus, ovaries, fallopian tubes, pituitary, adrenals, thyroid, chronic uterus area, diaphragm
Impotence	Testes, prostate, all glands, lower spine, diaphragm
Incontinence	Bladder, ureter tubes, kidneys, adrenals, lower spine
Indigestion	Stomach, liver, gallbladder, pancreas, intestine, sigmoid colon, diaphragm
Infections	Region of area affected, adrenals, Lymphatic System, spleen, liver, kidneys
Infertility	Reproductive System, all glands, lower spine, diaphragm
Influenza	Chest/lung, all glands: esp. pituitary, Lymphatic System, diaphragm, ileocecal valve
Insomnia	Diaphragm, all glands: esp. pineal
Jaundice	Liver, gallbladder, adrenals, thyroid, thoracics
Kidney Stones	Kidneys, ureter tubes, bladder, diaphragm, parathyroids, adrenals
Knee Problems	Knee/leg, hip/sciatic, pelvic area, lower spine, referral area: elbow
Laryngitis	Throat/neck, all toes, chest/lung, diaphragm, Lymphatic System
Legs (swelling)	Knee/leg, Lymphatic System, kidneys, adrenals
Leukemia	Spleen, Lymphatic System, liver, all glands
Liver Conditions	Liver, gallbladder, thoracics
Lou Gehrig's Disease	Brain, whole spine, all toes, chest/lung, all glands
Low Blood Pressure (Hypotension)	Adrenals, pituitary, thyroid
Lupus	All glands, intestines, liver, whole spine, diaphragm
Meningitis	All toes, whole spine, all glands
Menopause (hot flashes)	Reproductive System, all glands: esp. pituitary, adrenal and thyroid, chronic uterus area, diaphragm

DISORDER	REFLEX
Menstrual Cramps	Uterus, ovaries, fallopian tubes, all glands: esp. pituitary, thyroid and adrenal, lower spine, diaphragm
Migraine	All toes, pituitary, whole spine: esp. cervical and lower spine, neck, liver, diaphragm, intestines
Mononucleosis (glandular fever)	Lymphatic System, all glands, whole spine, diaphragm
Morning Sickness	All glands, diaphragm, stomach
Morton's Neuroma	Stretch the metatarsal heads, work around and then directly on the neuroma on both the plantar and dorsal side
Motion Sickness (land, sea, air)	Ear reflex, neck, cervicals, diaphragm, stomach
Mucus (sinus)	All toes, ileocecal valve, chest/lung, adrenals
Multiple Sclerosis	Whole spine, all glands, all toes, diaphragm
Myasthenia Gravis	Parathyroids, adrenals, brain, whole spine, neck, chest/lung, diaphragm
Nasal Polyps	All toes, all glands: esp. pituitary and adrenal
Nausea	Liver, gallbladder, stomach, diaphragm
Neck Tension	Neck, cervicals, lower spine, shoulders, all toes
Nephritis	Kidneys, ureter tubes, bladder, adrenals, lower spine
Nervousness	Diaphragm, all glands: esp. thyroid, whole spine
Neuritis	Reflex to the affected area, whole spine, diaphragm, all glands
Ovaries (ovarian cysts)	Ovaries, uterus, fallopian tubes, all glands: esp. pituitary
Paralysis	Reflex to affected area, all toes, brain, whole spine
Parkinson's Disease	Brain, all toes, whole spine, all glands, liver, diaphragm, chest/lung
Perspiring Hands and Feet	All glands, kidneys, liver, intestines, diaphragm
Phlebitis	Referral area: arm, adrenals, colon, liver, gallbladder
Pink Eye (conjunctivitis)	Eye reflex, all toes, cervicals, neck, adrenals
Pleurisy	Chest/lung, Lymphatic System, adrenals, diaphragm

DISORDER	REFLEX
Pneumonia	Chest/lung, diaphragm, all glands: esp. adrenal, ileocecal valve, Lymphatic System
Pregnancy	Reproductive System, all glands, whole spine, bladder, diaphragm
PMS	All glands, kidneys, Lymphatic System, diaphragm
Prostate Problems	Prostate, all glands, bladder, lower spine, chronic prostate area
Psoriasis	All glands: esp. thyroid and adrenal, liver, kidneys, intestines, diaphragm
Pyorrhea	All toes, all glands
Restless Leg Syndrome	Knee/leg, lower spine, hip/sciatic, pelvic area, shoulder
Ruptured Disc	Reflex to affected spinal area, diaphragm
Sciatica	Hip/sciatic, lower spine, chronic sciatic area, knee/leg, shoulder
Scoliosis	Whole spine, all glands, chest/lung, shoulder
Shingles	Whole spine, all glands, diaphragm
Shoulder Pain	Shoulder (top and bottom), cervicals, upper thoracics, hip, neck, diaphragm
Sinusitis	All Toes, chest/lung, ileocecal valve, adrenals
Smell	All toes
Sore Throat	Throat/neck, all toes, cervicals, Lymphatic System, adrenals
Sprain or Strain	Reflex to affected area, referral area to affected area
Spur on Heel	All around heel and directly on spur
Stroke	Tip of great toe (opposite side from paralysis), small toes, reflexes to affected areas
Sty	Eye reflex, all toes, cervicals, neck, adrenals.
Swelling	Lymphatic System, kidneys, adrenals, pituitary
Tachycardia	Chest/lung/heart, thyroid, adrenals, cervicals, thoracics
Taste	All toes, middle 1/3 of great toes
Teeth and Gums	Middle 1/3 of great toes, all toes, cervicals, neck

DISORDER	REFLEX
Tension (nervous)	Diaphragm, all glands: esp. thyroid, whole spine
Thyroid Problems	Thyroid, pituitary, adrenals
Tic douloureux	Neck, cervicals, parathyroids, diaphragm
Tinnitis	Ear reflex, all toes, cervicals, neck
Tonsillitis	All toes, Lymphatic System, adrenals, cervicals, neck
Toothache	Middle 1/3 of great toes, all toes, cervicals, neck
Tremors	Brain, all toes, whole spine, diaphragm
Tumors	Reflex pertaining to location of tumor, all glands: esp, pituitary
Ulcers	Reflex pertaining to location of ulcer: stomach or duodenum, diaphragm, adrenals
Uremia	Kidneys, adrenals
Urinary Trouble	Kidneys, ureter tubes, bladder, adrenals, thoracics, lumbar
Varicose Veins	Referral area: arm, adrenals, colon, liver, gallbladder
Vertigo	Ear reflex, cervicals, neck, all toes
Vitality (low)	All glands: esp. adrenal and thyroid, whole spine, diaphragm
Whiplash	Top and bottom of foot between great toe and second toe, whole spine
Wrist (sprain or break)	Referral area: ankle, cervical, upper thoracics, shoulder

A CONCLUDING THOUGHT
from "Stories The Feet Can Tell"

Let me remind you that Reflexology is a means of equalizing the circulation. We all know circulation is life. Stagnation is death. Everything around us that is alive is in motion.

Everything in the universe is governed by the law of motion, which is one of God's great infallible laws of nature. It is from the earth, sun and water which are constantly in motion that we receive our creative forces which are followed by growth, maturity and decay. Nothing stands still. Our vitality is either increasing or decreasing according to the quality and circulation of our bloodstream.

Study for a moment the life of a sturdy oak, which from a tiny acorn grows. Stop and observe how it lifts its leafy arms toward Heaven to receive from the passing breezes the exercise necessary to strengthen its root supply, increasing the capacity to gather moisture and nourishment necessary to furnish and keep the sap flowing freely through every part. If we cut off the roots sufficiently to rob it of its life-giving sap, how long will the tree be green and full of life?

In the face of this shall we forget the necessity of keeping our whole body in motion; every part in perfect rhythm.

It is my sincere wish that this technique of Foot and Hand Reflexology will stand side by side with other great therapy works in the onward march of science and progress.

EUNICE D. INGHAM

1938

INDEX

Reflexology

PULL OUT FOOT CHART ────────────►

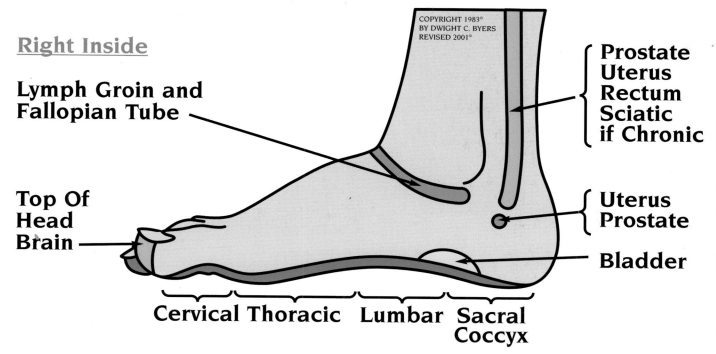

Right Inside

Lymph Groin and Fallopian Tube

Top Of Head Brain

COPYRIGHT 1983°
BY DWIGHT C. BYERS
REVISED 2001°

Prostate Uterus Rectum Sciatic if Chronic

Uterus Prostate

Bladder

Cervical Thoracic Lumbar Sacral Coccyx

Top Right

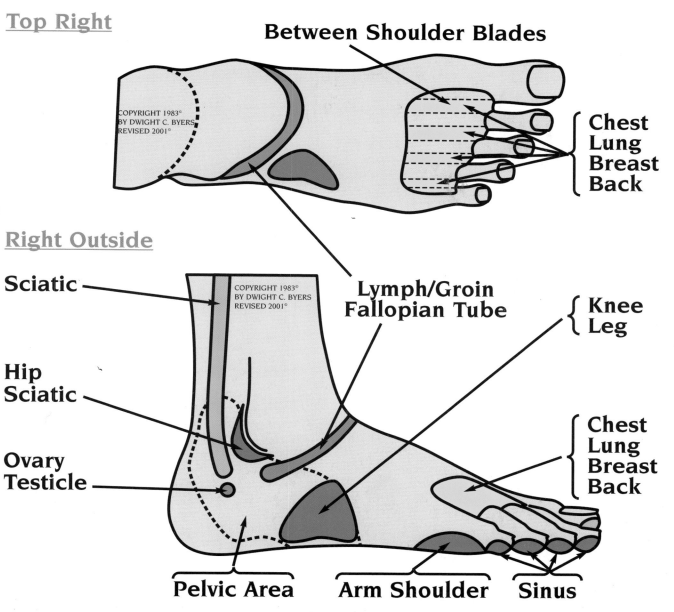

Between Shoulder Blades

COPYRIGHT 1983°
BY DWIGHT C. BYERS
REVISED 2001°

Chest Lung Breast Back

Right Outside

Sciatic

Hip Sciatic

Ovary Testicle

COPYRIGHT 1983°
BY DWIGHT C. BYERS
REVISED 2001°

Lymph/Groin Fallopian Tube

Knee Leg

Chest Lung Breast Back

Pelvic Area   **Arm Shoulder**   **Sinus**

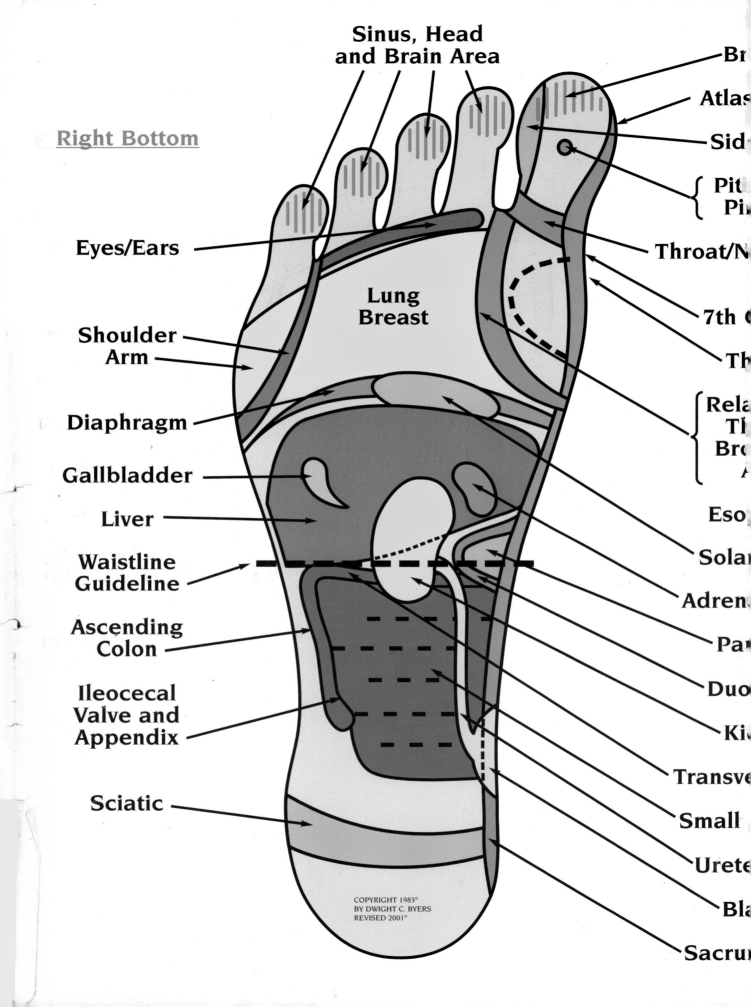

Right Bottom

Sinus, Head and Brain Area

Eyes/Ears

Shoulder Arm

Diaphragm

Gallbladder

Liver

Waistline Guideline

Ascending Colon

Ileocecal Valve and Appendix

Sciatic

Lung Breast

Br

Atlas

Sid

Pit
Pi

Throat/N

7th

Th

Rela
Th
Bro

Eso

Solar

Adren

Pa

Duo

Ki

Transve

Small

Urete

Bla

Sacru

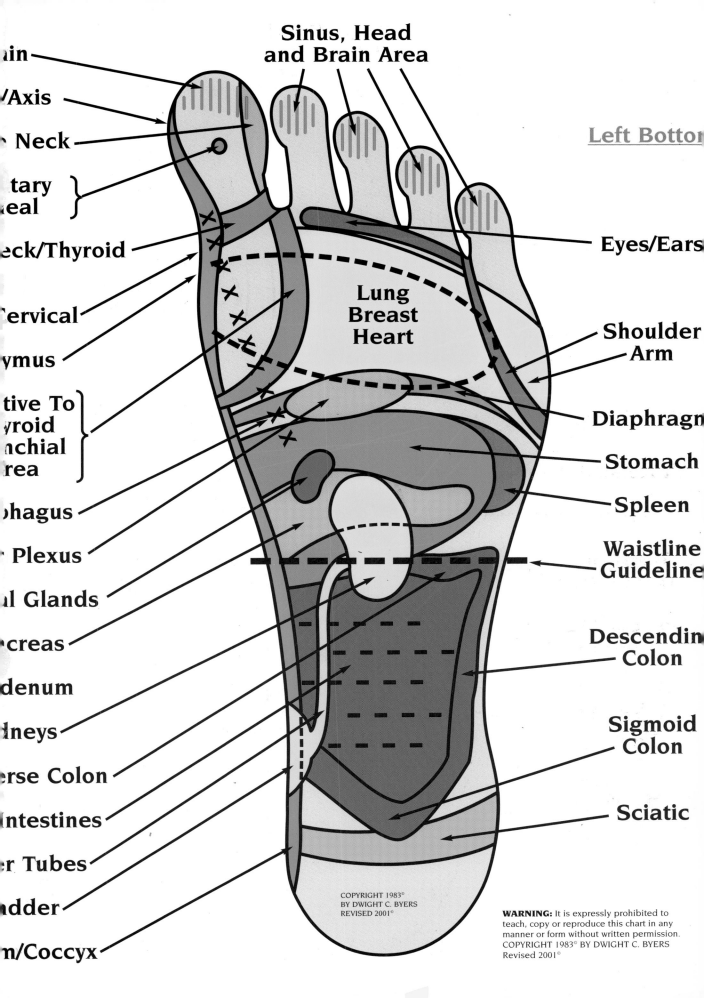

Sinus, Head and Brain Area

ain

/Axis

Neck

tary
eal

eck/Thyroid

ervical

ymus

tive To
yroid
nchial
rea

hagus

Plexus

l Glands

creas

denum

dneys

rse Colon

ntestines

r Tubes

dder

n/Coccyx

Eyes/Ears

Shoulder
Arm

Diaphragn

Stomach

Spleen

Waistline
Guideline

Descendin
Colon

Sigmoid
Colon

Sciatic

**Lung
Breast
Heart**

COPYRIGHT 1983©
BY DWIGHT C. BYERS
REVISED 2001©